TOWARD IMMEDIACY IN WORLD PEACE

TOWARD IMMEDIACY IN WORLD PEACE

Papers and Proceedings of the World Peace Congress

Thailand
July 9–11, 2010

Edited by:
Rajani Kannepalli Kanth, Padmamalini G. Rao,
Karen Ohnesorge and Tung-Yi Kho

Toward Immediacy in World Peace
Rajani Kannepalli Kanth, Padmamalini G. Rao, Karen Ohnesorge and Tung-Yi Kho

First Published, 2012

Published by
AAKAR BOOKS
28 E Pocket IV, Mayur Vihar Phase I, Delhi 110 091
Phone : 011 2279 5505 Telefax : 011 2279 5641
info@aakarbooks.com; www.aakarbooks.com

Printed at
Mudrak, 30 A, Patparganj, Delhi 110 091

This Volume, much as the World Peace Congress whose labours it embodies, is dedicated to the Women of this World who have, for Millenia, helped create and preserve the sancta of Peace and Accord in hearth and home that still endure. It is fondly hoped that they, in this Millenium, will extend, via vigorous entry into that world, that very same benefice to the public domain where men clash with each other daily, albeit driven by greed—or the desire to dominate.

Contents

PART IV: CONGRESS DOCUMENTS

Acknowledgements

The Governing Council of the World Peace Congress, the Trustee, and the Editors of this Commemorative Volume, acknowledge gladly and with gratitude the many who helped make this compilation possible ...

... For starters, the Thai organizers of the Congress, led by Rungnapa Surached, the Congress Patron, and Surasee Kosolnavin, the Congress President; next in line, the Authors of the papers represented here and the other Office Bearers of the Thai Congress, namely Trustee Rajani Kanth, Vice President G. Venkatesh Rao, Chair Anupma Sharma, Co-Chair Tung-Yi Kho and the Consulting Advisor Mahan Vir Tulli; further, the various Keynote Speakers, principally, Sulak Sivaraksa, Dhammananda and Art-Ong Chumsai Na Ayudhaya; the numerous panelists; the simultaneous translators, namely Darunee Kunchai, Wandee Tosuwan, Preeyaporn Srithai, Pramuansri Sripyan, Patsawee Arthan, Kamolporn Sirisoporn, Santi Srinin; the Volunteers who were Nongnapha Wongrajit, Kaisri Yotsuwan, Suebsakul Jaikla, Attaporn Hirunsirisombat and Noppadol Songsakaew; and the Participants, Visitors and Guests, who constituted the original Event itself. ...

... Also, the Hosts of the Royal Hills Resort, Pornpan Smuthkochorn, Vacharaporn Chokdeepanich, Kobkaew Chanaratsoporn and Tanaboon Chanaratsoportn, whose hospitality was the benefice on which the Congress was built. ...

... And the Videographers, Solarsin Ngoenwichit and Nalin Kittivech, who captured the Congress in moving images for all of us....

... And the Donors, Santi Bhirombhakdi, Julian Fryett, Sunchai

Trichit and ML Nanticka Worawan, for their generous support.

At another remove, thanks are owed the Aakar Books, Delhi, and its Publisher, Mr K.K. Saxena, and his skilled team of Printers and Editors, who helped produce the Volume, and the several personnel who helped translate the many Contributions from the Thai Language.

Finally, the special labors of Padmamalini G Rao, who first broached the idea of the Volume and subsequently labored, editorially-speaking, to bring it to fruition, ably assisted by Karen Ohnesorge.

It is to be hoped that this project serves a mission–World Peace–whose time, in these turbulent times of emergent political discord and economic chaos, is likely come.

•Preface

Caryn Mirriam-Goldberg

Cultivating Peace in Poetry

All over the world, everybody always strikes out at the enemy, and the pain escalates forever. Everyday we could reflect on this and ask ourselves, 'Am I going to add to the aggression in the world?' Everyday, at the moment that things get edgy, we can just ask ourselves, 'Am I going to practice peace, or am I going to war?' — Pema Chodron, When Things Fall Apart

There's no truer old cliché than 'Peace begins with me'. The way we work with our feelings of groundlessness, confusion, grief, anger and insecurity have a constant and direct impact on the peace we do or don't cultivate in our lives, and our lives, of course, on the lives around us. The pebble tossed into the water sends ripples that can effect the whole ecosystem of the pond for a moment or longer. The same is true with us.

When I was asked to provide a poem that would serve as a Preface for this edition of the Proceedings of the 2010 World Peace Congress, I started with the peace available to us in each breath, a way to inhale and exhale, staying with wherever we are at the moment, and how each breath is an arrival at a particular intersection of time and place, personal history and world events, the emotional weather coloring how we see the world and the economic, social and artistic weather of the world-at-large. I wanted to show readers and listeners how peace is available in simply staying with whatever we feel, what struggles we face, what critical moments scare or hurt us, what possibilities abound also. Arriving in peace so often means not departing for other distractions, such as turning the anxiety of being present with the hard moments into the distractions of aggression toward ourselves or others.

Pema Chodron, a well-known Tibetan Buddhist nun, writes wisely about this seemingly simple but lifelong lesson of how to stay with what comes. Staying means getting very familar with our habitual responses to feeling threatened by loss and pain. By understanding how we churn our fear and anxiety into limiting or even hurting ourselves, and silencing or avoiding others, we can better locate the pause button between pain and action. Once we learn to pause in that intersection, we have the opportunity to consider how to move, speak and be in the world in a way that fosters greater peace in our lives and the lives around us.

Peace at the intersections starts with us, taking whatever material life gives us, and staying with those materials enough to learn what to do with them.

The Crossroads in Every Step

We breathe in intersections, taking in here, exhaling there, memory and physiology, myth and heartwood, daring leap and long sleep—all right here at the crossroads. Take peace, for instance and always, how it unfurls from the lean edge of a branch, spreads itself into a recognizable shape, like leaf or what's left of the sky between leaves, and then, when it's time, hardens off, falls, flies, lands, turns into what feeds the tree. Nothing you can simply hold in your hand for more than a moment. Yet the air is different, easier to breathe, sharper in its brilliance. No place that's not an intersection. You're born out of two people's intersection, you die by entering deeply into another crossroads. No place that's not edge, no time that's not all times, what you've lived petaling out, what you're living rooting down. When the seasons tilt, and the land beneath you slides, so do you. The world is made of the glimmer between things, the light left by one for another, the dull shine of mid-afternoon on the driveway gravel, the irridescence of the car's reflection in the side view mirror. Giving peace a chance simply means arriving in the whirl of motion, the breath of give and take, the large light igniting itself at the intersection of wherever you are.

The World Peace Congress
History and Purpose

The **World Peace Congress** was instituted in Salt Lake City in 2007, holding its First World Congress, 24-26 August, and completing its set task of drafting Key Resolutions across three days of intense deliberations, that brought in activists, scholars, artists, politicians and lay people, to provide the basis for moving forward in its quest for world peace.

A **Second Congress** was held from 27 February to 1 March 2009, in Bangalore, India, consolidating this Mission.

The **Third Congress**, held in Thailand on 9–11 July 2010, followed through in embodying concrete grassroots projects scattered worldwide, the resolutions proffered by Congress 2007.

The *object* of these meetings is clear: to set up an institutional basis for co-respective and co-operative peace between peoples, unmediated by state, government or politics, understood in their traditional sense.

The *final goal* of these efforts is also equally clear: to achieve, as a binding precept, the *Universal Renunciation of War as a Means/ End of Social and Political Policy*, now and forever.

The **WPC** welcomes all those who share such a vision to join us in helping enshrine this idea via dialog, discussion and conversation, now and in the future.

Listed below are its broad ***Aims and Objectives***:

The purpose of the **World Peace Congress**, in the first instance, is to foster serious and immediate **dialog** between all the extant **paradigms/worldviews/interests/ideologies** that have divided the human world into disparate, and often feuding, **sectarian groupings.**

It is aimed, therefore, at nothing short of instituting a **permanent conversation** between **all** segments of the **human species.**

The dialog will be, thereby, between the varied **polarities** instituted by **geography, gender, ideology, ethnicity, language, philosophy, religion, culture and politics** (e.g. East-West, men-women, tradition-modernity, conservative-radical, north-south, etc.).

The object is to locate all possible **areas of agreement** that can serve to foster a **world-wide affiliation of peoples** who can, while maintaining and respecting difference, sincerely find **common cause** that will sustain the continued existence of planetary life forms under threat today by both **violence and greed.**

It will serve, we hope, in effect, to create the basis for a **union of peoples,** unattached to state, nation and power blocs, which will foster **ground-level action plans** geared to micro-initiatives locally, but fully informed of the **co-respecting spirit of human variety** as it dwells elsewhere, and everywhere.

It is hoped, thereby, to institute world-wide a permanent groundswell of support for **policies/actions of peace, non-violence and mutual nurturance,** in active resistance to the agendas of all those who seek to profit and/or rule at the expense of the **common weal.**

The Congress will adopt appropriate **resolutions,** both collectively and separately, in all spheres, including Plans for instituting **means, mechanisms and modalities** to realize them, in a consilient spirit of consensus, and establish the basis for future expansion of the **areas of mutual agreement** in ideas, visions and possibilities.

Congress Website: http://worldpeacecongress.info/

Patron's Note

Rungnapa Surached ('Tukta')

Along the path of life there are crossroads that become turning points. There were many times when it seemed as if I was at a dead-end, but friends provided the foundation and driving force for me to move on ahead in the right direction. Life's events teach me to face life with determination and strength. 'Giving' to others is deeply rooted in my heart and mind.

For many years, I did community work with good intentions but without a clear understanding of the nature of them. Disappointments soon followed. Then it occurred to me that work had become destructive. This realization stopped me from working for two years but I still thought about the 'correct' direction in which I had to proceed.

As noted above, with determination there is always a way out of seemingly 'dead' ends. Foreign friends, unheard of for nearly 20 years, of different nationalities, languages and domiciles, pointed the way to discover what I was looking for. The World Peace Congress was my start where I met diverse groups dedicated to building peace in small places and through cooperative activities.

My participation in the World Peace Congress 2009 in Bangalore, India, renewed my desire to do good. The exchange of ideas and experiences gave me knowledge and confidence.

As soon as I returned to Thailand, I began my participation in community works again. What I did were not new projects but old ones with a new approach. 'Harmony of Diversity' brings forth unity and strength. The important things are not structure, procedures or a perfect system of management. They are simplicity, understanding and connections within and between small groups in communities. Expanding connections creates forces necessary for success.

The return to community work is different from familiar ones of old. Every trip from Bangkok to the community felt like a homecoming. Meetings became talk amongst friends. Harmony-based on understanding moves community work along smoothly. Child development centers, mother and child care and alternative medicine programs, ecology-minded use of natural resources, comprehensive agriculture and forest planting projects were started by ideas hatched among the co-operation of community members.

What I learned from participation in the World Peace Congress goes a long way towards accomplishment of community programs and projects. It will be a good thing to pass the knowledge along to others. This was the motive behind the wish to hold the World Peace Congress in Thailand. At that time, I had no idea how to make arrangements for a successful Congress. All I knew was that it could greatly benefit community members and those interested in community work. The next step was to find as much information as I could to make my wish come true. The WPC Committee responded with care and full information. One month later, the WPC Committee informed me that the World Peace Congress 2010 would be held in Thailand. I felt glad and thankful for the opportunity.

The preparation for the World Peace Congress 2010 started, step by step. It lasted nearly nine months. Everyday people joined in, in ones and twos. The cooperation from people unknown to each other before but willing to move towards the same destination together heartened me a lot.

At last came the World Peace Congress 2010 which ended successfully as planned. But friendship goes on, bringing exchange of ideas, experiences and cooperation. Peace expands, little by little.

Lastly, I would like to thank all the people who helped make the World Peace Congress 2010 possible. Thank you.

President's Note

Surasee Kosolnavin

Imagine all the people living life in peace. I am greatly pleased that, finally, the report of the 2010 World Peace Congress (WPC) has been accomplished. The Congress brings together prominent leaders, thinkers, religious leaders and civil societies' activists from all over the world to discuss ways by which people with various backgrounds can foster a sense of peace.

I do believe that the timing of our gathering could not be more timely. The world we live in is increasingly becoming more and more unpleasant. The atmosphere has become more depressing as the world continues to witness the rage of wars, conflicts and violence.

Some might even characterize the present world as a much more dangerous place today than yesterday. For this, one should only look to what is happening in many states in the world to find a reason why the world is facing such tremendous stress.

Indeed, the WPC is intended to provide a venue for concerned citizens of the world to share their thought and wisdom, discuss practical ways to enhance cooperation and eradicate prejudices and foster deeper mutual understanding among different civilizations. This might sound too idealistic, but we should never give up hope. The light of hope is often preserved through a consistent effort by the enlightened few.

Therefore, it is our hope that the WPC can continue for years to come.

Finally, as President of the 2010 WPC, I would like to thank everyone who generously supports the WPC, for their hard work in making the WPC a great success. I do hope that this report will disseminate thoughts, ideas and recommendations that came up from the session in Nakhonnayok, Thailand and enhance our commitment to ensuring the primacy of peace over conflict.

Vice-president's Note

G. Venkatesh Rao

Among the esteemed dignitaries on the dais, delegates from various parts of the world, friends, other participants and invitees ... I stood deeply humbled and touched by their gracious presence at that august gathering, assembled for the purpose of making our universe, our globe, our world, our countries and our communities a better place to live in, free from the scourge of war and the ills that come with it.

Prof. Rajani Kannepalli Kanth, in his most profound and deeply perceptive speech during the Congress, analysed the progress of mankind as an enlightened group constantly yearning for greater achievement but failing to comprehend the significance of renouncing war as an instrument of state-craft. Violence, translating itself into an organized force and resulting in war, can never bring about a lasting to solution to any dispute; it can only postpone it. Therefore, he advocates that nations must amend their constitution to include a pledge, a promise a conscious decision that they will not adopt war as a means of resolution of disputes with their neighbours and others in the comity of nations.

The simple truth and pragmatism of the saying of H.G. Wells has not been comprehended by the advocates of war, who fail to understand his words: 'If we don't end War, War will end us.'

The advancement of modern technology has reached a stage where our superpowers and many other powerful nations of the world have developed nuclear and other weapons which can annihilate the human race and the entire planet earth several times over. The kind of suffering and death that will be caused to all living creatures and mankind is unimaginable. Wars are no longer to be viewed as mere regional conflicts between nations who are unable to resolve their disputes through peaceful means. Albert Einstein famously said, 'I know not with what weapons World War III will be fought, but World War IV will be fought with sticks and stones.'

In the history of civilization, numerous wars have been fought;this has brought about untold misery on both the families of the victors and the vanquished as invariably there are casualities on both sides, hundreds of thousands of soldiers and civilians die, and large numbers suffer injuries and become disabled for life in the war. Innocent civilians—often, large numbers of women and children who are not connected with the armed conflict—have to often bear the brunt of aerial and long distance attacks.

Prolonged warfare, lasting several years, results in peoplebeing unable to lead normal lives asthey are constantly living under war psychosis, thereby permanently damaging the psyche of a nation. These nations are unable to reconcile themselves to the psychological effects of war and conflict whichare carried further to several generations, thereby perpetrating war mongering as an instrument of state policy in many nations.

Mahatama Gandhi rightly observed: 'If we are to teach real peace in this world, and if we are to carry on a real war against war, we shall have to begin with the children.'

Therefore, we have to begin with the children of the world so that the next generation in all nations is adequately taught to emulate the most noble and enlightened apostles of peace.

Apart from Education, spreading the teachings of peace and massive international campaigns advocating the cause of peace and the renunciation of war, serious efforts have to be made to bring about renunciation of war as an instrument state policy through international law. We must use law as an instrument of change towards bringing about acceptance by the various nations of the world, by reaching out to them through various international organizations like the United Nations and its other allied organs.

We must try to coordinate and cooperatewith various other international and domestic non-governmental agencies in bringing about the necessary pressure and focus to urgently attend to the menace of war which threatens to annihilate the entire planet. Billions and trillions of dollars are being spent on stockpiles of weapons. These funds can be diverted and utilized towards the betterment of humankind, eradication of hunger, poverty and disease. The other equally serious ill-effects, namely global warming and pollution which threaten the planet, can also be controlled.

Therefore, it is only through education, propaganda, people's pressure and legislation that we can bring about the renunciation of war as an instrument of state policy. The landmarks in the development of international legislation, treaties and agreements which prohibit and have contained nations from going to war have their beginnings in the writings of Hugo Grotius, also known as the father of international law—namely his famous treatise, The *Law of War and Peace* (1625) andsubsequently *The Peace of Westphalia* (1648), a series of peace treaties defining the various parameters of relations between nations and the manner in which peace could be achieved between various warring nations. The subsequent creation of the International Red Cross (1864), the First Hague Convention of 1899 and the Second Hague Convention of 1907, the Treaty of Versailles and League of Nations (1920), the Kellog-Briand Pact, the Geneva Convention on POWs, the creation of the United Nations (1945), the International Court of Justice, International Criminal Court, the Universal Declaration of Human Rights, all the Nuclear non-proliferation treaties, and treaties relating to chemical and biological weapons, etcetera, are all landmarks of Global statesmanship at creating the necessary framework and diplomatic channels for dispute resolution, prohibition of weapons of mass destruction and creation of alternatives to armed conflict and war.

There is no doubt that mankind has evolved to understand from its terrible experiences of two world wars that war is no longer a viable solution to dispute resolution among nations; yet, mankind is unable to completely renounce war as an option. It is here that the leadership provided by the World Peace Congress will help the the nations of world to make final permanent efforts in bringing about the renunciation of war on our planet.

And finally I would like to conclude by quoting the wise Chinese philosopher ...

> To put the world in order, we must first put the nation in order; to put the nation in order, we must put the family in order; to put the family in order, we must cultivate our personal life; and to cultivate our personal life, we must first set our hearts right. — *Confucius*

I have no doubt that the World Peace Congress will achieve its purpose and goals very shortly and each one of us will be lighting the candle that would light up the whole world, and bring about lasting peace and brotherhood in mankind.

I thank you for giving me an opportunity to share my thoughts with all of you.

Chair's Note

Anupma Sharma

I am an entrepreneur and social activist from India.

I came to the Congress as a learner, with an inner calling to create, contribute and establisha system for a whole generation of peace makers. I had no great design or big plans. However, witnessing the participation and enthusiasm at the Congress, my journey, since, has been charted by a commitment to relentlessly accelerate the process of peace, adding further to my commitment to support and crusade for 'meaningful intervention' in building peace.

I would like to acknowledge the support of the participants and very capable organizers, who have been responsible for the Congress' success. Everyone will agree that it was an experience which we will not forget.

We had some wonderful outcomes for and from our young participants, some real challenges and, of course, contribution in the form of resolutions discussed, thought out and drafted by every single panel of very capable participants.

It is through this data that we can see some of the real outcomes of the partnerships between all ofus, stakeholders.<para>I believe that 'intent for peace' is the single most needed good action in today's world for bringing peace to the individual life and, at the same time, for playing a larger role in the achievement of global peace.

The World Peace Congress must play a pivotal role of ensuring the different stakeholders across all sections of the societal spectrum work together to ensurea better outcome for the present and the future. We see some real successes in this area.

Of Particular Note are the resolutions presented by the panels.

In the panel, 'Gender and Patriarchy', panelists came to the conclusion that everything begins at home. What we see in the outside world is merely a reflection of our individual lives. We cannot expect to change anything around us unless we practice thesame at the bottom of the pyramid or the foundation, if I may say so, in our own homes and lives. This brings us to the core of it all—women, who are, however discredited, still the designers ofhuman life. The unfortunate reality is that this very component of life and the world at large is largely neglected and subjected to unimaginable injustices across the world regardless of region, class or culture.We can achieve little if women's issues are not addressed and rectified. This can be achieved by encouraging participation of women in decision making at all levels, beginning from home.

In the panel, *Politics and Militarism*, peace scholars tell us that peace has in fact, been the dominant human experience and that war—rather than the rule—is an aberration in human affairs. Nor is war very old. War becomes possible with the advent of territoriality about 10,000 years ago and begins to develop with the rise of cities about 5,000 year ago. More people die of hunger across the world than because of war. However, the focus, monetary and otherwise, of various states lies on militarization. If nations wish to have peaceful relations, they would have to encourage de-militarization and disarmament, while pursuing trade, diplomacy and international law as guarantors of peace. Can we one day establish a global union that will abolish war and secure human rights for all? Of course we can! This is no pipe dream. Peace has existed for thousands of years and we are only now beginning to learn the power of nonviolence as a solution to war. Our best days lie ahead. There is hope!!

I feel that being instruments of change isn't attributed to any real or imagined qualities, but to the understanding that peace is a part of life. There has never been a time when each person's thought activity has been as important as it is today. One human being's thoughts, whether he or she is emitting light waves of love and sincerity or dark waves of egoistic desires, can move humanity either toward complete peace or devastation.We also work for the simultaneity of life and believe that excellence in the process of peace is a lifelong discipline, and has to be linked with both personal and social responsibilities.

My efforts for the future include encouraging a support and connect between peace crusaders and seeing implementation of the mission and purpose of the Congress to make it an effective, potential force for relevant intervention, emerging from within the resolutions passed by the Congress.

This note would be incomplete without specific mention of Ms. Rungnapa Surached for her relentless efforts for months in making the Congress a success. At the conclusion, we can be very proud of what we have collectively achieved. I would like to sincerely thank the participants from all across the world and the organizers for their time, expertise and input. We rely on them to foster the connect with community members in their sphere of influence to effect change, better practices, opportunities and outcomes for the purpose of this Congress.

I would also like to thank the panelists for their great support of the Congress and their willingness topartner across boundaries to provide better outcomes. I thank them for support and expertise.

Lastly, I would like to thank KhoTung-yi, Co-Chair, for his great efforts. As many of you would know, he participated under adverse personal circumstances. It had been a very difficult time for Tung-yi and I would like to thank him for his professionalism in ensuring the operation of the Congress was maintained and that we met key commitments.

At this point, a note of heartfelt gratitude to Professor Rajani Kanth, Congress Trustee. I thank him for steering and guiding us on the path of peace!

We have many challenges moving forward but also opportunities to make a difference to the lives in and around our individual worlds. I hope you will continue to support us to achieve this.

If you fling all of your thoughts into these simple words, and, from this moment keep living your lives anew, before you know it, your individualistic or cliquish feelings will diminish, and you will feel yourselves wishing for the happiness of mankind, with a feeling of humanitarian love welling up from within. Gradually, the individual's character will approach wholeness and the person's lifestyle will strike a harmonious note—which is the greatest thing an individual can do for world peace.

Therefore, I encourage us all: through purposeful contribution towards world peace, let the original blueprint for a peaceful world be carried out to perfection as soon as possible, with the least amount of suffering. I would like to ask each one of us to contemplate this truth, and to join in the movement for world peace through dedicated effort.

Co-chair's Note

Tung-Yi Kho

The 2010 WPC meeting in Nakhonnayok Province, Thailand was the Congress' third. I feel extremely privileged to have been involved with the movement since it began in 2007, when the Congress was inaugurated in Salt Lake City, Utah, USA. A second meeting was held in Bangalore, India in 2009.

I should note that while such a chronology is able to convey the times and locations of the Congress as historical facts and, hence, to evoke a certain sense of accomplishment, it tends to belie the challenges the Congress organizers have invariably had to encounter prior to each event. And what challenges! Perhaps they serve to highlight the very real difficulties that confront the quest for peace; or perhaps they underscore just how precarious or elusive peace really is. In any case, any feeling that our mission has been accomplished is surely premature, if not misplaced.

Apart from the usual concerns about funding, our preparations for Congress this time around were complicated by the fact that Thailand was mired in violent civil conflict just weeks leading up to our July meeting. The decision to go ahead with the Congress was, in fact, made at the height of the conflict, when a section of downtown Bangkok had become a war-zone, set ablaze by rampant gunfire and explosions. Furthermore, there was a looming threat that the chaos would spread to other parts of the country.

Even now, with the benefit of hindsight and the distance of time, our decision to continue with the Congress still seems like one fraught with considerable risks, particularly when foreign embassies were urging their citizens to stay away. However, the Congress Steering Committee felt that the circumstances and their immediacy affirmed the *raison d'etre* of the WPC: if there was ever a need for a peace congress, perhaps it was here and now! So, following consultation with our Thai colleagues, who closely monitored developments on the ground, we decided to proceed.

It is indeed rare for us as ordinary citizens to pursue common-good ideals such as world peace; the burden of realizing such 'lofty' aspirations is widely assumed to fall on national governments and the various state-oriented multilateral institutions. Even when these institutions have proven to be woefully ineffective in addressing such concerns, there remains a real lack of grassroots people-to-people initiatives committed to resolving human conflict on a global scale. The tendency in recent human history has been to conceive of ourselves (and others) along the lines of nationality, citizenship, caste and creed. This has unfortunately bred insularity along those same lines. Indeed, it has become increasingly apparent that the modern condition is one that generally militates against human solidarity, and against notions of the 'common' and the 'collective', with all their attendant implications for the future of humankind. The intervention of the World Peace Congress, here, is apt and timely. It represents an attempt to reclaim our role as global citizens responsible for safeguarding peace and human security on a global scale.

Thanks and congratulations are therefore due to all who came to Thailand and partook of this fledgling process. It is my hope that it was a meeting that inspired all in attendance the wish to further the cause of world peace. Special thanks must go to our gracious hostess, Ms Rungnapa Surached, without whom the Congress would not have taken place: she went beyond the call of duty to raise the funds necessary for our meeting. I would also like to thank Ms Anupma Sharma, who at short notice willingly accepted the responsibilities of Congress Chair. Finally, I would like to acknowledge the Congress Trustee, Professor Rajani Kanth, whose vision and tireless commitment to the cause of peace has given us the WPC in its present form today.

About the Contributors

Art-Ong Jumsai Na Ayudhaya serves as Chief Administrator of Sathya Sai School, Lopburi Province. Dr. Ayudhya served as Senior Lecturer of The Faculty of Engineering at Chulalongkorn University; Member of Parliament (Elected three times); Senator of Bangkok; Secretary to the Foreign Minister; and Expert in the National Research Council on rockets for use in the Artificial Rain Making Project. Dr. Ayudhya received Ph.D. from Imperial College of Science and Technology, London University, U.K.

Kampanad Bhaktikul is an Associate Professor at Mahidol University with teaching and researching interest in environmental conservation. He also teaches natural resources conservation at Irrigation College, Kasetsart University. Kampanad also teaches at Southeast Asian Studies Programme, Thammasat University to follow regional biodiversities and the changes in Mekong and Salween Development. With internal practice, Kampanad has been invited to draw the subject on "Geography for Peace" at Arsomsilp Institute of The Arts, the alternative university in Thailand reflecting world searching for "loving and living with nature" peacefully.

Pongthorn Chanluen is Director of Projects for New Male Health Care (M Plus), Chair of the Rainbow Sky Association and a representative of the Gender Diversity Network, Thailand.

Sornchai Chatwiriyachai is a former engineer and management school professor who left that life behind to pursue his passion in drama in education and life-long learning about life itself. Sornchai is probably one of the first persons who brought "Theatre of the Oppressed" techniques to Thailand to enhance political awareness in Thai society. His spiritual quest brought him to Buddhism. He now facilitates unorthodox group works using dialogue, drama and dharma to help people re-connect to their Buddhist roots in a new way.

Bikkhuni Dhammananda, Chatsumarn Kabilsingh, was born in 1944 to Voramai Kabilsingh and Kokiat Shatsena. Her mother, Voramai, was the first Thai woman to be fully ordained as a *bhikkhuni.* Chatsumarn Kabilsingh relates how her mother became a nun when she (Chatsumarn) was ten years old, but rather than leaving the home as most women do, Voramai turned her home into her temple. Chatsumarn received Buddhist instruction and training along with the nuns. She says that her father, Kokiat, was "the first Thai man I knew who strongly supported the revival of the *Bhikkhuni Sangha* in Thailand." Unusual for Thai women, Chatsumarn received a higher education. After high school, she received her B.A. in Philosophy from Visva Bharati University, her M.A. in Religion from McMaster University in Canada, and her Ph.D. in Buddhism from Magadh University in India. She married, has three sons and three grandchildren. She taught for over thirty years at Thammasat University in Bangkok, Thailand, in the Department of Philosophy and Religion. Dr. Chatsumarn Kabilsingh is a well-known author of many books on contemporary issues in Asian Buddhism, including Buddhism and Ecology and Women in Buddhism. She has often said that she knew she would become a monastic in the Buddhist tradition at some point in her life; she was just waiting for the right time. That time came in 2000 when she took early retirement from Thammasat University and received the bodhisattva's precept from Fo Guang Shan in Taiwan. In 2001, she took her lower ordination in Sri Lanka from Ven. Bhikkhuni R.Saddha Sumana and Ven. T. Dhammaloka (bhikkhu). In 2003, she was ordained a full *bhikkhuni,* also in Sri Lanka, the first Thai woman to be ordained in a Theravada monastic lineage. Her *bhikkhuni* name is Dhammananda. Her ordination lineage is Syamopali from Dambulla chapter. She currently resides at the Songdhammakalyani Monastery in the Muang District,

Nakhonpathom province, Thailand. Since her ordination, the Ven. Bhikkhuni Dhammananda has written several books, designed to educate the public about various issues related to Thai Buddhism, including the place of women.

Ritu Datta was born and brought up in a middle class North-Indian family fed on high ethical values. Creative from an early age and a happy go lucky person, Ritu has worked in the field of media as researcher, writer, producer and director for more than a decade. Initially trained in India and later abroad, she has been nurtured by renowned filmmakers. A freelance writer for print and electronic media, she has conceived and written educational scripts for national radio and National TV programmes. Her documentary films include an interesting body of work related to social issues and the arts and culture of India. Her films have won wide acclaim from artists, viewers and media critics. She is well known for her unique and original approach to her subjects. Humanity is her religion; she is always ready to extend a hand for any noble cause and has a passion for learning. She is an eternal student.

Rajani Kannepalli Kanth has held affiliations with the United Nations, Columbia University, the State University of New York, the University of Utah, University ofAarhus, Denmark, University of Texas, Austin, the University of New South Wales, J. Nehru University, The University of Technology, Sydney, Providence College, Wagner College, Washington College, Bard College, The University of Bielefeld, University of Bremen, the National University of Singapore, Oxford University, Duke University, Tufts University, and Harvard University, amongst others. His various published works include Political Economy and Laissez-Faire (1986), Explorations in Political Economy (1991), Capitalism and Social Theory (1992), Paradigms in Economic Development (1994), Breaking With the Enlightenment (1997), Against Economics (1997), Against Eurocentrism (2005). His newest work is titled The Challenge of Eurocentrism [N.Y.: Macmillan (2009)]. Fellow of Harvard University, currently, he lives in Salt Lake City.

Tung-Yi Kho is a doctoral candidate in Sociology. His research interests span the natural sciences, the social sciences, and the humanities. He is currently researching how and the extent to which Eurocentrism takes root in contemporary China's experience of modernity with a particular interest in their implications for the future of humanity. The Congress's Secretary General, he also served as Co-Chair of the Thailand Congress of 2010.

Surasee Kosolnavin is former Chair of the National Human Rights Commission of Thailand; he served as President for the 2010 Congress in Thailand.

Seema Luitel is from Nepal and is trained as Sociologist with a Masters Degree in "Sociology" and also a Masters in Science (Gender and Development) from Asian Institute of Technology, Thailand. She also has a Post-Graduate Diploma in Children, Youth and Development from ISS, the Netherlands. Her areas of expertise are in Social Development and Community Mobilization, Children, Women and Youth Issues, and in matters dealing with Peace and Conflict. More recently she has been the Director of a project titled "Peace Building from Below", funded by CIDA (Canada). This project is a conflict sensitive development project, being implemented in two conflict affected hilly districts of Eastern Nepal. Since the project responds to the post conflict context, the project has used Gender Equality & Social Inclusion (GESI) strategy and Peace Conflict Impact Assessment (PCIA) tools to promote peace and reconciliation at the community level.

Prasert Meetam received his training in mathematics and serves as an assistant professor in the Department of Mathematics at the Prince of Songkla University in Thailand. He has written extensively on energy policy and social issues.

Caryn Mirriam-Goldberg, a poet, writer, teacher and facilitator, explores and celebrates how the spoken, written and sung word can inspire our lives and communities. Founder of Transformative Language Arts at Goddard College, where she teaches, she is the author of eleven books, and a long-time writing workshop facilitator and performer. She is the 2009-2012 Poet Laureate of the State of Kansas, USA.

Karen Ohnesorge is a poet and artist whose central themes are compassion, spirituality, radical love, and social justice. Her research considers how artists and writers put image and text together to question ideas about race and gender. She currently serves as Dean of Instruction for Ottawa University, a small liberal arts college in Ottawa, Kansas, USA.

Padmamalini Rao is an editor with Tata-McGraw Hill Education, Noida, India. Her working career includes editing Social Science texts and school textbooks, teaching Middle and High School Level English and French and marketing, integrated circuits, and satellite based electronics. Her early life, including school and college education, was in Bryn Mawr, Pennsylvania, USA; she now lives in India with her husband, an Advocate in the Supreme Court of India, and her two sons. She is a practicing lay Buddhist and a member of Soka Gakkai International in India, working with youth and educators to promote faith-based and value-based solutions to modern challenges.

G. Venkatesh Rao is an Advocate at the Supreme Court of India for the last 23yrs, and has specialized in various branches of domestic and International Law. He has had vast experience with Constitutional law during his tenure with the Office of the Attorney General. He has appeared in numerous cases of national and International importance having implication and relating to constitutional law issues. He has also defended several legislations of the Central and State Government in India which were challenged in the Supreme Court of India.

Anupma Sharma is a Motivational and Lead-by-example Manager with over 17 years of experience in International Marketing; Business Planning , Event & Media Management, and Social Activism, especially in the field of Empowerment of Women. She served as the Chair of the Thailand Congress of the World Peace Congress in 2010.

Sulak Srivaraksa has been nominated for the Nobel Peace Prize and received the Right Livelihood Award and the Gandhi Millennium Award. He is the founder of the International Network of Engaged Buddhists and more than a dozen other international organizations. Born in 1933, the year Thailand emerged from absolute monarchy into democracy, his life has been intimately bound up with Southeast Asia's modern history. He was a Buddhist monk for two years, and then completed his higher education in Great Britain, where he also worked as a writer and commentator for the BBC. He is the intellectual voice of his generation in Asia, best known for his indefatigable efforts to bring people together into community, common work, and a shared vision of a more enlightened world. Sulak is author of *Seeds of Peace: A Buddhist Vision for Renewing Society, Rediscovering Spiritual Value: Alternative Consumerism From A Siamese Buddhist Perspective, The Wisdom of Sustainability: Buddhist Economics for the 21st Century* and more than 100 other books and monographs. He lives in Thailand.

Phra Thanomsing Sukosalo is the President of Dhammadrops foundation (DDF). Following in the Buddha's path, he is a young monk who works with troubled children from schools and juvenile detention centers. Last year he and his students walked from Chiang Mai to Nakorn Prathom (over 700 km) without bringing food and money. During this trip, they also declined offers to ride with motorists to experience how easy and happy life can be without consumption.

Rungnapa Surached, "Tukta," is the director of Sports Marketing Group, Singha Corporation, Thailand. She is deeply committed to using her work as a means to promoting youth and community development. She has assisted with a number of community projects throughout the country and at present, is working closely with a number of village communities in Northern Thailand toward becoming more economically and ecologically sustainable.

Nuttarote Wangwinyoo has spent most of his life in search of how to live life fully and harmoniously with others. He works for environmental justice and the conservation of head water forest and culture with indigenous people in Northern Thailand. He also facilitates dialogue sessions for people in the government or corporations to really and deeply hear each other. His passion in education always brought him to work with teachers at all levels to explore a way to empower self-learning and self-determination.

Trustee's Address

Rajani Kannepalli Kanth

Hi, Everyone: *Sawat Dee*!

I address you now in extremely trying, and portentous, times, to put it mildly.

We are, in my opinion, at one of the great CrossRoads of History.

A way of Life, that I call *Modernism*, bequeathed to all by European Conquests of the past Four Centuries is, slowly, coming to an unannounced close.

That much is clear.

What is less clear is the nature of the New Societies that are to emerge from this systemic, spontaneous breakdown of the *Ancien Regime.*

But that may well be their defining *logos*: that they will be Autonomous, Diverse, even Multivaried.

And they will *not* be under the Hegemony of European Domination.

And that is why, I fear, Crisis is inevitable.

The existing Hegemons will not allow diversity to exist, if they can at all help it.

In fact the history of European Expansion is the history of the virtual, and systematic, extinction of *all* societal modes contrary to *Euromodernism.*

It is a Project that is still extant.

And a weakened set of Hegemons may be even more dangerous than Strong ones.

Indeed, the Doomsday Clock is set now, as you might know, . at Six Minutes to Midnight.

Hence, my friends, this Peace Congress: so we can review the nature of the Challenge(s) before us.

*****

But Global Politics and Economics are not the only take on this matter.

So, let us approach it from another angle.

What is our own culpability, as *individuals*, for tensions in this world?

It may appear that we, the Masses, are innocent.

Not so.

Our daily lives in Civil Society are about Competition and Struggle: for *Survival.*

In effect, so-called Civil Society is a Jungle: and like a jungle—it is insecure.

Listen, perchance, to even casual commuter conversations in the Modernist world.

Every one is complaining about someone, or something.

So, simple *conflicts of interests* keep us tense and vulnerable, and prone to anger, frustration and, above all: *Mutual Distrust.*

It is the Quintessential *Hobbesian* Condition: bequeathed us by our European Patrons: in the name of Progressive Modernity.

So the Modernist Ethos itself is destructive of Cooperation, and Pro-Social, Communitarian behaviors.

And that is just in Everyday Life, quite apart from the routine power struggles of Politics, and the State.

Which is why we need this Peace Congress.

To understand How we Live, and Why.

*****

So far I have spoken about Hegemony and Conquest, by States and Governments, as the reason for holding Peace Meetings, here, there- and everywhere.

I have also spoken of Daily life in Civil Society that stokes such tensions on an Inter Personal level

But does this mean that outside of Hegemony, Civil Society, and Modernism, such Problems cannot, or do not exist?

They do.

So now let me turn to the most Ubiquitous source of Aggressive Tensions in all Societies on this Planet.

It inhabits, indeed, virtually half the Human Race.

It is the nature of Men : and *Masculinity.*

To state matters bluntly, Men are endowed with the instinct to Kill, and Women with the instinct to Nurture.

Yes, *instinct.*

It is not a word that fits easily in Modernist Discourse because they are all into Species Denial.

Yes, *Species Denial.*

Which is why, *e.g.,* their Economics is not about *Needs*: but *Wants.*

Needs imply Organisms, *Living Entities.*

Modernism prefers to use *mechanical* metaphors for us.

To place this in context :recall that we 'humans' are, contrary to Judeo-Christian and other religious Mythologies, are *animals*: Apes, or Hominids to be precise, sharing over 95% of our Genes with the former.

And some of us still think we are created in God's image!

Some god!

So we are part of the Natural world, howsoever we cloak ourselves in the trappings of Culture, Myth, and Ideology.

This is the real threat : *We are the Source,* or rather *Men* are: - of all Violence on this Planet that is human in inspiration.

So, the Permanent basis of Violence is *Indelible,* because Men, in their collective aspect, are possessed of it.

Civilisation, which is, in my definition, simply the Domestication, or the *Pacification of Men,* only goes so far: but, sadly, not far enough, to erase this .

So, Capitalism and Empire—which are real enough—are not the *only* forms that produce systemic violence; though they certainly instigate it 'rationally', and calculatedly: but the Male portion of so-called 'Human nature', that is the Eternal Provenance of Conflict and Wars—Big or Small.

Wars are not about Right or Wrong, despite the usual Propaganda: they are about *Men fighting Men,* over any pretext that is handy.

And Revolutions are about *Little* Men challenging the rule of *Big* Men: Until it's *vice versa* again!

In Human society, there is, sad to say, an *Iron Law of Oligarchy*, and an *Iron Law of Patriarchy*, as well.

This is a sobering thought: and I place it before you advisedly.

Of course, our well-funded '*social scientists*' pledged to be troubadors of the system will deny this, for, they will tell us, we live in the best of all possible worlds.

And that is why we need this Peace Congress

To make us Self-Aware.

To help see through their Spin.

*****

Let me sum up the foregoing.

In a nutshell, Violence exists amongst us because of Ruling Elite Power Struggles, Modernist Alienations [which includes both Capitalism and Socialism], and the everpresent baseline Drives of *Masculinity*.

To state it, collating these propositions, succinctly: Male Drives for Domination and Greed create, daily, a world of *Intermittent Violence.*

What then is the Antidote?

How are we to Countract it?

Well, Nature is, perhaps not accidentally, *double-edged.*

It created Men: but also *Women* - with a rival, but radically different *species -being.*

Yes, Women are contrary to Modernist pretences, different from Men.

Indeed, the Promise of Civilization is given by the very existence of Women.

The Material Economy, of Greed and Power is a Masculine one; but the *Moral Economy* of Sustenance, and Cooperation is *Feminine.*

So the few *Hospitalities* that exist in all societies, that allow life to continue, is perennially given by the existence of women.

Indeed, the very Provenance of *Morality* in our Species is given by the *Species Need—vested in women*—to ensure that the Human Child, amongst the most vulnerable of all Species, can be reared safely to maturity : secure from the Predations of Men.

So it is that Nature assures the Continuance of the Human Race.

And that provides us, providentially!, an Existential basis for Hope: and that hope vests, inexorably, in women.

And so we are holding this Peace Congress:

To *Empower Women* to sue for Peace, so the world may be preserved for All.

*****

But there is More.

Contrary to the make-up of European Modernist Civil Society, there have been and still are, Social Formations that are relatively free of its '*bellum omnes contra bellum*' *Hobbesian* Correlates.

By far, the Greatest Single Alternate is simple,'Tribal Societies where Kinship provides the Cementing bond pacifying the predations of Men, to a large extent.

The Tribe is an *Extended Family* within which Violence is, potentially, limited.

As such, the Natural allies of Women are Tribal Societies, free of elaborate social stratifications.

Societies like the Bushmen and the Aboriginals have a lot to teach us in this regard.

For they too subsist within what I have called a '*Moral Economy*'.

So now we have *Two* Natural Antipodes to our Modernist Wasteland: Women and Tribals.

Already, Male dominated Modernist societies start to look like a pathetic minority!

But there is more.

Peasant Societies are also *Subsistence*-oriented: and thereby exist on the active periphery of a *Moral Economy*: think for instance of the Chiapas, and the rebellion there against NAFTA, a fairly typical Peasant Initiative, actions repeated throughout the period of Modernist Revolutions.

So that's another dormant, occasionally eruptive, *Third* Force.

Finally, Industrial Workers: in particular, those of them who are still close to their Peasant Roots share similar premises.

And that's a very large *Fourth* Force.

Let's take Stock.

Women, Tribals, Peasants and Workers, all share common characteristics: of living in a Needs based Moral Economy, in part, or in whole, voluntarily or involuntarily.

And they far outnumber the Profit driven, *Consumerist* Societies of today that are the Agents of War and Commercial Expansion; indeed, recall that both the World Wars of the last century were wholly Modernist in inspiration.

This not merely augurs *Hope*, but virtually guarantees it.

So I am happy to tell you all that, with the gradual rise to Self Knowledge of all these Forces, in our Times, and before our eyes, I have named today, the Long Era of Modernist Conquistadores is almost at an end.

And hence we meet at this Congress:

To disseminate this insight, and support Native Peoples, Peasant Societies, and Working Communities, reject the imposition of alien and alienating institutions devoid of their affirmation & consent.

*****

There is still one Last sliver of a very real Hope.

We are, as Humans, incurably *Tribal* in our psyches.

It is our Herd mentality.

And we are *Totemic*, also, in our attitudes.

So we—*and in particular Men*, follow Leaders: for better or for worse.

We saw that with Gandhi: regrettably, also with Hitler.

Millions were ready to sacrifice themselves, at but a nod from the Great Man.

So Charismatic leaders can, at least to a point, lead us away from Instinctual drives.

From Routine.

From Habit.

From the Prison of Material Reason.

It is my belief that such Leadership will arise now: for the Planet, a Living Entity, has need for it.

In Human Society it is ever the *Few that lead the Many.*

So here is a *Fifth Force* that can help us achieve our aims.

That's not too bad, really : given that that is one more than the (Four) Forces of Nature that guide the entire Cosmos!

*****

So we are here not merely to erect Barricades against Warmongers, but also to help understand and configure the Societies that will, I believe, replace them.

This is a Long Road: and we stand but at its humble Beginnings.

The First Step is to ask all Governments on Earth *via* Political and Non-political action to alter their Constitutions to *Outlaw* War as a Policy Tool.

In tandem, this Congress must write to the SG of the UN to call for such a Universal Declaration of the Renunciation of War.

My, that really sounds good; but it is actually even better than it sounds.

Now, the Modernists will not join us here.

They will see us as Idealists or, worse, *Utopians.*

For they are seriously mistaken about the nature of Human Reality.

Modernists are unaware that the world is first created by Dreamers: and then expropriated by hard-headed, practical people.

The Taj Mahal must first be *imagined,* before it can be built.

So dreams come first, always.

So it doesn't matter if the Modernists don't join us.

For Women will.

And Tribal societies will.

And Peasant organizations will

And Workers will, for the most part.

And a *new* Brand of Leaders will.

Now that's a Lot of Voices.

Indeed, they form, I am happy to say, an Absolute Majority of the Human Race.

So, I would like this Congress to spread this vital Message all across the World:

That We, the WPC, stand committed to Peace and Peacemaking.

That we stand committed to Renouncing War – and Violence - as means of Statecraft.

That, further, we stand committed to forswear Violence in Speech, Thought and Action, as far as humanly possible.

That all International Issues, much as domestic issues, need to be resolved Bilaterally, and Peacefully, without External Intervention and Force.

That *Great Reconciliations* are yet possible between even the bitterest of enemies.

For you see we Humans, in their *Tribal essence*, are, ultimately, a *Consensual* Species: and chafe at both Majority and Minority rule.

The Great John Stuart Mill, venerated Patron Saint of Modernism was *wrong*: *we must not 'force people to be free'*.

No, Force is always wrong.

Issues resolved by Force and Fiat are *unresolved* by *counter forces* at some future point: which is why politics is always r*eversible*.

But issues attested by Faith and Consensus, like *authentic cultures*, endure forever.

So the Means are as important as the Ends.

People *qua* people, do not wish to be ruled from above: only to be left to pursue their respective Autonomies, albeit within their *cultural* domains.

The Modernist Nation-State, a European innovation, is an artificial, imposed entity held together by economic, ideological, and military force.

But, contrary to EuroModernism, real Anthropic Society is not a contract between interested parties, but a balance of *affections*..

Indeed, let me ask you turn now to the Human Family, to learn from that remarkable institution.

The Weak herein often have Strong Voices, occasionally, even Veto powers.

Ever seen kids pulling protesting parents into a toy store? You get the picture!

Why?

Because a human Family is an Emotional Entity, based on Sentiment.

Not a contractual, rational entity as Modernism defines, and deforms it., as *e.g* with Modernist definition of Marriage, and society itself, as a *Contract.*

As a Balance of *Interests.*

It is Not.

It is a balance of *affections, of emotions, of loyalties.*

Note also that Members of a Family are *Not Free, not Equal, Not Democratic.*

But it is yet a haven, for all of us,, because it is based on Caring and Co-operation.

Warmth.

It's the same with *real, Anthropic Society*: it is also based on *warmth.*

You see we are all *Mammals,* heat seeking animals: whereas the EuroModernist has turned us into *Reptiles,* cold and calculating cadavers.

Which is what European *Civil Society,* the Model being exported under Globalisation, today is: *heartless.*

In that charming model, you can sell your mom on Ebay: and if she protests, its likely only because the price is set too low!

I am joking, of course, but the real life struggle today is between the Mammals and the Reptiles.

This is a valuable insight and leads us to the idea of the Sovereignty of *Shared, emotive* Communities: not aloof States and Governments ruling over Economic and Military Empires where our lives are fragmented into being solely ' *producers and consumers.'*

We are defined by Neither: we are human beings whose greatest preoccupation is to huddle, not accumulate or consume.

As I said, we are heat seeking, not light seeking, animals.

This idea is little short of a Revolution in the History of Humankind.

So we are here to make History: and Peace.

And hence this Congress.

That's why I am here: hope you will join me, not some day, in the remote future, as John Lennon sang, but here, now, today.

Let's do it: let's ask the world to awake from its protracted, dogmatic slumbers.

Blessed are the Peace Makers, it is said.

So be it, at WPC 2010.

In Thailand.
Today.
Now.

*****

Now some of us, perhaps many of us, even most of us, may be skeptical of such Lofty Aims.

I respect Skeptics: for they are Rational - they want Facts, Proof: not high Rhetoric.

So I say to the Skeptics: there is only *One* way to demonstrate that we are on the Right Road here.

And that is by joining us: and working toward such Ends.

For we are not Soothsayers who predict the future, rather, we are Activists who engineer it.

For you see the True Realists are those that Demand the Impossible.

As they did in the recent past: when they demanded Universal Suffrage, Votes for Women, or Civil Rights for Minorities.

It is such strivings that make the apparently impossible, *probable.*

It will never be a Perfect World for each of us, all of us, are Imperfect in some regard.

So the only Option we have is to demand, *i.e. Petition* and Struggle for such Amenities.

Day after tireless day.

Yes, they will, as Gandhi said, first ignore us, then laugh at us, then possibly even fight us: and then, thereafter, we will, surely, prevail.

Given our tribal nature, vast majorities are not needed.

It take but One to start a Movement, Two to constitute it, and Three to Consummate it!

And this struggle itself will need to continue, as a continuous process,, even if States can be pressured to Amend their Constitutions to Renounce War.

Eternal vigilance will remain the price not merely of Liberty: but also of Peace.

So let us not dwell on why such Aims are difficult.

Of course they are!

Let us strive instead to help reduce the difficulties, one tiny baby step at a time.

Walking on the moon, if it happened at all!, was *not*, sorry Mr Neil Armstrong!, a Giant Leap for *Humankind.*

But *Renouncing War* will be somewhat more akin to that.

And ensuring that the Means of War are banned will be the next, follow-up step.

We may be *beginning* this struggle with Words, but we will consummate it with Deeds!

And that's why we need this Peace Congress; now, in the future, and, perhaps, for evermore.

So please join me in this Journey of a Thousand Steps that has taken the world Millennia to evolve to this point.

For, today, We are the World, *galvanized.*

And we will, together, write its Histories to come, simply by making them.

But how shall we make them at the WPC?

Our Objectives, as defined in 2007, are Clarity itself.

Let us all put our heads together to invent, create, and concoct simple, generic projects that embody our common humanity and that can be presented to warring groups, anywhere and everywhere, by way of enticing them to participate in some small enterprise, without fear of compromising their separate stances even whilst still feuding.

The idea is to establish *human contact between Adversaries*, no matter how preliminary, so both sides, all sides, can learn that their enemy is not so different from them.

Our effort is to build bridges between the many, and isolate the few who make, and benefit from, War(s).

For example, perhaps Women on both sides of a War, may join hands in pushing for mutual restraints during wartime.

I will not say more: for I would much rather you pondered this counsel and applied your own creativity to it.

So we are here to Imagine the Ways and Means to bring Peace to the world, unchecked by both conventional wisdoms - and fallacies.

*****

One Important Caveat.

We are all Opinionated Folks.

It follows, since we are thinking people.

And so we, *ipso facto,* loathe those whose opinions are different from ours.

Let us try at this Congress to avoid that very human impulse.

The Human world is diverse: All Types exist.

We need to figure ways of being able to *Converse* with the Other.

So I welcome All to this WPC- even Warmongers and Imperialists.

So we can talk, and talk, and talk: instead of fighting.

So That's why we need this Congress: to keep All Adversaries talking.

*****

In closing, let me thank you all for coming here, at prohibitive cost of Time and Expense.

For you are the WPC, in Action.

Let me first, at the very top, recognise the gracious Madam Tukta Rungnapa, who is our Host for this Event, and whose contribution to the WPC is simply immeasurable.

And Mr Kho Tungyi, the Co-chair of this Congress, for his valiant labors for over a year to make this possible. Indeed, he has been with the WPC since 2007. To me, he is Mr WPC.

Next, Ms Anupma Sharma who Chairs this Congress, a fearless crusader for many of our objectives, most of her life.

And Mr. Surasee, the highly modest President of this Congress: and Mr Venkatesh Rao, the equally unassuming Vice President.

All of us, and all of the above, have made this a Historic Day: and we haven't even gotten started yet!

So the best, you see, as the adage goes, is yet to be!

Thank you all.

I wish you, I wish us, all: *bon chance!*

We have not the luxury of failing: so we have no option—*we must succeed.*

Albeit, One Congress at a time.

And we will.

Kha Kun, & Chok Dee!

Keynote 1

Bikkhuni Dhammananda

Your Highness, Your Excellencies, Your Holiness, Sisters, Brothers, and Friends of the Earth ... I am a newcomer to this organization. Before coming, I made some enquiries from some Thai people if they had heard of this Congress. They said Oh, they had heard of this Congress being held here in such a luxurious place like this. They doubted very much if we could achieve anything out of it. I personally was also afraid that we would eventually end up joining one of those NATO conferences: NO ACTION, TALK ONLY.

But given a second thought, the organizers emphasized very much the importance of our attitude ... that it is our own making: this Congress is our responsibility ... mine as much as yours, to make it work.

I trust it will, with our clear guidance, a divine guidance.

No, I am not talking about supernatural power ... simply *that* guidance, which comes through the clearest state of mind based on compassion for sentient beings.

The Uniqueness of the Truth versus Buddhist Teaching

If I tell you I am going to talk about the essence of Buddhist teaching, it might turn you off if you are not Buddhist. So let me talk about the uniqueness of the Truth and eventually I will bring you to the understanding of the essence of Buddhism. So you will get two in one.

Before Buddhism came into existence, Brahmanism talked about the existence of self which is eternal and unchangeable. The Buddha denied [refuted] that self which is eternal and unchangeable. Rather, this is what he proposed: that which is, is not permanent and is changeable.

As you walked in a few minutes ago, are you the same person or not the same person? Yes, and no. Medical knowledge provides us with the fact that the cells in our body keep changing all the time. We do not get old all of sudden but, when we reach 25, the decline has begun. So, Dhammananda who walked into this hall some minutes ago is, in fact, different from the person speaking to you right now. This is the truth. Yet, because there is continuation of the existence of Dhammananda then and now, that is why you call me, this form, this body, Dhammananda.

This basic fact that Buddhism talks about is not only true for Buddhists but for everyone. That is why I said this is the uniqueness of the Truth that it is applicable to all of us.

Because now we are talking about something that is applicable to all of us, there is that common interest.

Peace talk starts from this common interest ... from the understanding that things are changeable, that nothing remains eternal [comes the understanding that] if we are in conflict, it can be changed, it can be improved. It is up to our commitment.

Another related truth: things are interdependent. Look at our body. It is composed of the four elements: earth, water, air and fire. Each element cannot be by itself; it is interdependent and interchangeable.

And our life depends on this balance and interdependence of these four elements. Buddhism talks about this; but then, it is not true only for the Buddhists. It is true for you and me as well.

The realization that we are interdependent, ethically make us humble. I have to care for you as much as myself. I have to care for your nation as much as mine.

These four elements within us are related directly with the four elements of the universe. Now we see ourselves as part of the universe (comparatively we are just a minute particle in this universe).

Peace cannot be limited only to human beings; peace must be applicable to our environmental surrounding as well.

With this approach, we see that the whole universe is nothing but a complete whole which is all related and interconnected.

We cannot talk about peace from within without caring for peace at large.

Our commitment is not for us only as individuals, but for communities, and for the universe.

Having given you my understanding of Buddhism and the larger context of the Truth, yours and mine, I now move to speak in a more specific context.

Wearing the garb of a monastic, whether I like it or not, I am making a statement. I am representing my faith ... that is, Buddhism. You might not be aware that women do not have their ordained status in Thailand, but it was the intention of the Buddha that Buddhists consist of *bhikkhus* (ordained men), *bhikkhunis* (ordained women), lay men and laywomen. These four groups or fourfold Buddhists are to work as the foundation for Buddhism. We have been instructed to study his teaching and put it into practice, then defend it, should the occasion arise.

When I went forward to receive ordination in 2001, yes, I had to go to Sri Lanka for it, as they do not (yet) ordain women in Thailand. Upon returning home, there was much protest from the traditional conservative Buddhists.

I went through a period where I had to find peace within yet, struggle to barely survive ... alone. There were two factors responsible to see me through the difficult time. I thought it might be of some interest to share this with you at this august gathering. One, ordination was given by the Buddha. I trust him completely that it is the best path for me and also for many committed women. The key word here is TRUST. I trusted that this young prince became enlightened at the age of 35. Since then, he has been known as the Buddha, the Fully Enlightened One. I trust also that the enlightenment was not for him alone, but that it is a message and that he was the living proof that it is for us equally. Ordination is a short cut to it. I trust him in his supreme spiritual goal that it will work for me as well.

Two, we have a phrase in Pali which says *'Dhammo ha ve rakkhati Dhamma carim'* Dhamma protects one who practices it.

To draw from my own case, and apply it to our search for peace, trust is the key word underlying our commitment.

We gather here as a group, coming from various parts of the world with different cultural and religious backgrounds. We must share the same trust ... that Peace is possible and we are actualizing it in our commitment.

Peace and Conflict

When we are peaceful, it is an accepted fact and there is no need to talk about it.

When we start talking about it, it implies that peace is missing from our society and we miss it, so we yearn for it. We do not talk about peace without conflict. So when we start talking about Peace, we are already in trouble; we are already in conflict.

Let us be participatory. Allow me to try a simple idea on you. Let us talk with body language. Please raise your hand and give me three fingers.

Do you see the differences? Some of you give me three as in the middle finger, ring finger and little finger. Some of you give me the index finger, middle finger and ring finger. And yet, you could also give me your thumb, index finger and middle finger.

All read the same 3.

Yet there are differences.

Do you realize that with the difference of giving me your three fingers, it implies some cultural differences already? By expressing which three of the fingers tells us the differences in our geographical backgrounds.

Now let us continue to play this game a little further. Give me one finger please.

Most of you give me your index finger—that is the most common and accepted as a message for 'one'.

But I am also giving you the same message of one with my middle finger—you all laugh. You see, your reaction is based on your reading of the second layer of meaning of this middle finger.

But, from my point of view, I am giving you the very first meaning of it—that is, the message of one. But you are reading it with the second layer of interpretation, which is your cultural interpretation which I do not have. Taking it for granted that the middle finger implies the second layer of meaning, you would get angry at me but I am so naïve, I do not have that second layer of the meaning.

Conflict begins.

I am offering a simplified example of understanding or misunderstanding which comes from entirely different sets of interpretations. Without understanding each other, and not realizing that we are using different sets of meaning to the same language or body expression, this is how we get ourselves in trouble.

I speak convincingly as I learnt it in my own life. When I started running the temple, my community consisted of women of all ages, coming from different educational, cultural backgrounds. After two years, I realized I was not making sense either to myself or to them. We did not understand each other's language. I used to get terribly upset and annoyed. Now realizing it, I always make it a habit to allow them to tell me their understanding of what I said, and show me if they have really understood it. Eight out of ten, they still don't.

The peace process should begin here. Make sure that we are using the same set of understanding. Words alone do not work. We need workshops. We need the space to make mistakes together and see each other's mistakes, and to correct each other, and love each other in that process of learning.

Let us be less wordy, and more action [oriented].

My last point is on equal gender participation.

I do not believe in gender equality per se. Yes, I believe in equal opportunity for both men and women to participate in various activities in life, in society, in our countries. But men and women are basically different; we should come together and put forward our best.

In one research study, women have proved to be more adept in 18 skills out of 24, whereas men have only 12. This is why I never wanted to be equal to men, which means I am lessening my already acquired abilities. Allow us to think together, plan together and then work separately according to our ability. Opening up the space for women means you are respecting your mothers, wives, sisters and daughters who are half of the world's population and because they take care of our children, they are the ones who hold the responsibility for the future of the nation.

You can talk so much about Peace, but unless women are included in this thinking and planning process, if there is peace at all, that Peace does not last.

Now I come to my concluding part.

The first letter in Peace is P: for **participatory.**

The second letter is E: for **equality.**

The third letter is A: peace has to be accessible at all **levels.**

The fourth letter is C: Peace must have the keyword of **compassion.**

And the last one E: Peace must be like **elephant.**

Let me explain about the elephant. In a Thai saying, men are compared to the front legs of the elephant and the women are the hind legs. Traditionally, it implies that the women should always follow the men like the hind legs always follow the front legs of the elephant. What happens if the hind legs decide to sit down? Can the front legs take the elephant forward? So, the last letter, 'e', representing the elephant, is gender awareness, the emphasis on working together—the male and the female.

Thank you for your kind attention.

Keynote 2

Sulak Sivaraksa

We are not in a *post*-imperial age since the American and the Chinese empires are rivaling for (global) domination—often in collusion with transnational corporations, which own and/or control the mainstream mass media and educational institutions. These forces are also promoting militarization through arms production and sales, et cetera. Consumerism prevails and capitalism is considered the only game in town. Even nominally communist states such as Vietnam and China are beating many capitalist countries in the very game of capitalism. India has abandoned its non-alignment—once a source of its pride—and has caved in to American domination. To cite some random examples, the Thai kingdom as well as Pakistan, the Philippines, and Indonesia have long been subject to these forces and structures.

I should like to refer to Bruce Rich's *To Uphold the World: The Message of Ashoka and Kautilya for the 21st Century.* Most people do not know about Kautilya, who was the brain behind Chandragupta, grandfather of Ashoka, who defeated Alexander the Great in India. Rich claims that Kautilya is much more subtle than Machiavelli and the world is now following Kautilya subconsciously; that's why violence and deceit are the order of the day. Rich pleads that if we turn to Ashoka for nonviolence, this will really be the way to uphold the world in the twenty-first century.

Likewise, we hear a lot about violent conflicts, ecological disasters, market exploitation, massive and growing income inequality, and so on. But we hardly hear about movements for self-rule and emancipation. They are growing confidently and quietly, often building on the legacy of *satyagraha* (the power of truth) and *ahimsa* (nonviolence).

When a tree falls, there's a lot of noise. But no one hears a tree when it grows.

Once, the Gross Domestic Product was considered the standard and the universal measurement of economic and social wellbeing. Now Gross National Happiness is increasingly gaining wider acceptance—with Bhutan, Ladakh and Kerala serving as paradigmatic examples.

Traditionally, economists saw their main task as largely about generating economic growth. They played (and still do) an influential role in the World Bank, IMF the WTO and in almost every government. In recent years, however, there have been many high-profile defections from the camp of economic orthodoxy such as by Amartya Sen, Joseph Stiglitz, Jeffery Sachs, et cetera. They rightly feared that mainstream economics would drag the world and its inhabitants down the precipice of destruction. Likewise, last year, the organizers of the World Economic Forum annual meeting in Davos, Switzerland, invited the Buddhist monk, Matthieu Ricard, to deliver a keynote address on Gross National Happiness.

In summation, the tree of alternative economics is growing gradually. It all began with E.F. Schumacher's Buddhist economics more than three decades ago. Perhaps Buddhist economics is now strong enough to weather the storm of mainstream economics. A think tank at Schumacher College has joined hands with the New Economic Foundation in London, propagating the idea that Buddhist economics be taught at the university level, especially in the economics faculties of mainstream universities.

Politically, the way forward requires refraining from seeing and deploying violence as a means to an end—as the US is now doing in Iraq and Afghanistan, China in Tibet and Xinjiang, the military dictatorship in Burma, et cetera. Like Aceh, the three southernmost provinces of the Thai kingdom must be granted a greater degree of self-rule. There's no way other than nonviolence.

Mahatma Gandhi employed the power/politics of truth in the form of *satyagraha* to struggle against and expose the lies of the British empire. China still resorts to falsity to deceive its people. But now there is book titled *Prisoner of the State: The Secret Journal of Premier Zhao Ziyang*. Although the Chinese government banned the selling of the book in the country, it is widely available. The book exposes the deviousness and mendacity of the Chinese Communist Party and the author has expressed support for students' and people's movements for democracy. In China, the websites and blogs revealing the truth and giving relevant facts and information are also proliferating despite government control. As such, the deceitfulness of the ruling class cannot last for long. Strikes by the labour movement in China are now widespread despite despotism in that country. This is a good sign.

Fidel Castro argues that although he came to power through arms struggle and revolutionary means, he condemns mindless violence and prefers nonviolence. Despite decades of American terroristic activities against Cuba, Castro still believes that the American people are friends of Cuba and sees young Americans' tilt towards nonviolence as a move in the right direction.

President Ramos Horta of Timor Leste also upholds the virtue of nonviolence and forgiveness. He is willing to forgive and even cooperate with Indonesia despite the latter's bloody invasion and occupation of his country. He relies on the example of South Africa under Nelson Mandela, who was ready to forgive the crimes of apartheid. The former president of Indonesia, Abdurrahman Wahid, also declared that Gandhi was his political role model.

At first sight, the prime minister of Cambodia appears to be a malicious person who is trigger happy. But we tend to forget that the Dhammayatra movement also originated from Cambodia. It was founded by the late Maha Ghosananda (aka the Mahatma Gandhi of Cambodia) and is still a vital and influential force in the country. We can also refer to Buddhist monks during the so-called 'saffron revolution' in Burma who struggled for democracy and responded to the military dictatorship's 'counter-revolutionary' brutality with deep meditation and prayers. Likewise, Tibetan monks and lay people have been nonviolently resisting Chinese occupation for many decades.

Parallel developments can be seen in the academic world. To give some random examples, there are many books following the trail blazed by Schumacher's Buddhist economics. Then there's Glenn Paige's *Political Science without Killing* and David Loy's *A Buddhist History of the West: Studies in Lack,* not to mention the works that have come out of the Mind and Life Institute under the guidance of the Dalai Lama.

World peace links directly with self-rule which is a form of personal practice and transformation—the creation of a new subject. It requires internal/spiritual changes that constitute and are constituted by three external dimensions, that is, economic, political and intellectual independence. If one is able to transform greed into generosity, hatred into loving kindness and delusion into wisdom, that is really self-rule. Peace in the world requires the simultaneous cultivation of seeds of peace within. As the Dalai Lama pointed out, this is a terribly difficult process, but it is the only way towards peace.

Keynote 3

Art-Ong Jumsai Na Ayudhya

Peace has to start with the individual; you cannot have it, you cannot create world peace without individual peace. So how are we to find peace in life?

We all say 'I want peace' and the answer is in those words 'I WANT PEACE'. If you want peace and nothing else, you have to get rid of two words: 'I' and 'WANT';then you are left with the word 'PEACE'.

'I' is the ego or attachment to oneself. When people say bad things to us we become angry because of our ego. In this world, today, we like to compare the 'I' with others and so we become jealous and angry. Get rid of the 'I' or the ego; then we don't need to compare ourselves with others. Then we will be happy.

You have to get rid of the word 'WANT' also. These days, we live in an age of consumerism: we want more and more of everything. We are consuming a lot of energy that is available in this world. In 35 years, we won't have any more oil. After 15 years, we won't have any more natural gas in the gulf of Thailand.

We are searching for peace; you can't find peace from light, sound and all the places thathave light such as nightclubs—that's only the excitement of emotion, which can't last long.

There is a story about a lady who lost her needle. She was searching for it under a lamp post in the middle of the night. Some boys and girls were passing by and they asked the lady what she was looking for. They helped the lady look for the needle but could not find it. Then they asked the lady where she had lost it. The lady said she had dropped it in her bedroom, but the bedroom was very dark so she came to find it under a lamp post as there was a light there and she could see everything clearly. When the children heard this they laughed and told the lady to go back to her room. She had to go and find it where she had lost it, not in other places. In the same way, we have lost our peace from our hearts, so we cannot go and find peace in nightclubs or in other places of entertainment. We have to go back to our hearts; then we will find the peace that we are looking for.

We are all very fortunate to be living in Thailand where we have a very wise king who has taught us the principles of a 'Self Sufficient Economy'. Learn to be self sufficient and sustainable. We have to learn to reduce our desires and our wants. The more we want, the more disappointment we will have. With less want, there will be less disappointment. If we have no wants, then there will be no disappointment and we will be full of peace and happiness.

Whatever we think, so we become. This is the power of positive thinking. Learn to see good, hear good, speak good in everything that we do. When we use our ears to hear, why is it that we get upset or angry when people swear at us? Let us consider this in a scientific way. What is it that is entering our ears? It is simply vibration of air consisting of oxygen, nitrogen and carbon dioxide. Neither oxygen nor nitrogen nor carbon dioxide can make us angry. Thus when people swear at us, we say to ourselves it is only vibration of air. So we need not become angry with anyone.

In the same way, when we see something bad, let us consider it scientifically. What is entering our eyes? It is simply a form of energy that we call light or electromagnetic waves consisting of vibration of electrical field and magnetic field. There is nothing bad in the electrical and magnetic waves. Thus if nothing bad comes into our eyes, but we still see something bad, it shows that everything is in our own mind. Learn to see good in everyone and in everything. When you have a problem or an obstacle in your lives, be happy because, we need problems to learn how to solve problems; we need obstacles so that we can learn to overcome them and so we can go forward more quickly.

We should all learn to still the mind and calm the mind. This will give us a lot of peace. Do not allow anything to disturb the peace that we have gained. Learn to practice meditation as this will give us better concentration so we have greater efficiency in our work. It will increase our memory and improve our work efficacy.

Finally, we should learn to love everyone and all things. We should practice loving kindness or compassion. Having found some peace in our lives, we should help everyone to find peace also. We should be a good example to others.

May the whole world be filled with peace always.

Panel I: Gender and Patriarchy

Pongthorn Chanluen

Introduction

This panel address responds to a reality in our society where the father's gender is considered more important, even though some may say that being a father is not the only responsibility of a male who is generally called 'father'. Within the paradigm of this patriarchy, our society still believes that the world consists of only two genders, which are female and male. In the biological context, it may be explained that a person with two X chromosomes is assumed to be female. A person who has one each of X and Y chromosomes is then called male. This is a traditional interpretation of biology 'fact' that is used to hold up a society which, in a circular fashion, has assumed that there are only male and female.

However, in terms of sociology, there are other issues that need discussion apart from chromosomes or physical perspectives. For instance, a person who was born a female might not want to be called a woman or might not behave like a typical woman. On the other hand, a person who was born as a male might consider himself—or *her*self—as some other gender identity, such as a man who dresses like a woman, a homosexual man, a transitional woman or a cross-gender woman. However, society seems to allow them to 'perform' themselves—in other words, to live out their lives openly as persons with these other gender identities—only in limited spaces, for reasons of bias, beliefs, knowledge and understanding. Instead, they are restricted to living in their small, private societies, because they risk vulnerability everywhere else. These restrictions make it difficult to access accurate information. At the same time, the social atmosphere for simply talking about gender status still entails difficulty: those who speak frankly might be condemned as being rude or filthy.

Historians like Linda C. Bing Glossy North (Linda Schiebinger), and Thomas La Curtain (Thomas Laqueur) have discussed the differences between the male and the female in the physical sense. They have mentioned that the construction of 'women' and 'men' on the basis of differences in biological characteristics has been a Western way of thinking since the eighteenth century. In the previous century, Europeans had perceived females and males to be the same gender and understood that the male and female sex organs were not completely different—believing that the male sex organ had merely been further developed than the female. Medical studies in the early eighteenth century mainly focused on the similarity between male and female sex organs rather than the differences.

However, by the middle of the eighteenth century, this concept was replaced, highlighted and emphasized with the idea that all female and male body parts such as the sexual organs, the skeleton and brain systems were entirely different. One could conclude that historical social challenges faced those who sought to create new knowledge, and these challenges were constantly changing. It seems that each new understanding of gender status has been gradually developed with both positive and negative social impact. Strong reactions are not surprising, since new knowledge of gender seems, over time, to degrade the power of a man-dominant society or patriarchal system.

In Thai society before the year 2003, sexual diversity was not well understood; sexually diverse people were mostly referred to as homosexuals (probably meaning both male and female). Current Thai language for describing sexual diversity is much more complex. Familiar words such as 'Ga-teay' (hermaphrodite) can be used on both sexes but is more commonly used to describe males who act or dress like females. 'Tut' and 'Tutsy' both mean gay males who act or dress like females. Some words are used non-judgmentally, based on a characteristic or identity, but the meaning of words such as 'Ga-teay', 'Tut', or 'Tutsy' will depend on the tone and behavior of the speaker; speaking in a higher tone than normal, or with aggressive and sarcastic overtones, will make the words insulting and disparaging. 'Ga-teay' means *third sex*, a phrase that has become less popular because it suggests lesser value among the sexes. (Males and females also try to avoid the numbering of the sexes to avoid the issue of who came first, whether it's male or female.) 'Ga-teay' is not a Thai word, but rather a Cambodian word meaning *otherness* or *the minority*, or *marginal people*, depending on the interpretation.

The point here is that society tries to categorize its people using many criteria, such as sex, gender and sexuality. The hierarchical categorization system puts 'male' in the first place, then 'female', then 'Ga-teay' (according to Thai society's arrangement). Putting 'male' in the first place suggests the value and importance of males in Thai society, which can be observed in many situations in society, even in religious matters such as ordaining female Buddhist monks (Bikkhuni). Thai society is still a patriarchal society. Executive and management offices are also patriarchal arenas. 'Ga-teay' can rise up to the management offices, but they have to cut their hair and become a 'man, ' changing their 'feminine' personalities into male to resemble their birth sex, because having a feminine personality will conflict with their introduction as a man and can be damaging to the (patriarchal) image of the company. This situation is apparent in Thai society, or even the use of the phrase 'second type girl' which degenerates these individuals' value and human dignity, in being seen not as the 'first type girl', which is being female by birth, but being seen rather as female by artificial means. Some people might still like the term because at least there is the word 'girl' in it, thinking that, though they cannot be a real girl, at least they can be a 'fake' girl. Unfortunately, this might become a trap within their beliefs. The old beliefs try to categorize and evaluate people according to tradition and customs.

Traditional beliefs and social attitudes are essential mechanics that support patriarchal society. Utilizing language to control and manage society is a specific expression of violence in the society, because every time this method is used, it is a type of branding that assigns value and judgment to the subject. For example, the phrase 'HIV Prevention Project for Homosexual Males' is meant to help us understand behavior and health issues, but instead is used to oppressively determine the identity of a group of people who are homosexual males.

Society is assigning more importance to the identity of sexual or gender minority groups. This change could be explained through grand narratives. The old male/female dichotomy was the thinking way of the 'Century of Ideology'. Now, patriarchal systems and their traditional ideology should recede gradually. In the coming century, gender equality is not limited to female or male but will include those who have a variety of emotions, feelings, sexual lifestyles and sexual satisfactions. From now on, our society may adopt a new definition which is not focused only the female, the male and the homosexual. We have to explain gender differences on the basis of our understanding of gender and sexuality in order to reduce gender bias in society, and we have to offer a method of thinking which is able to convince people to recognize the latent oppression that sustains a patriarchal system. Therefore, the scope of 'sex' would unite with 'Gender Status and Sexuality (Sexual Identity)' with important consequences.

Gender Status and Patriarchy in the World of Ideology

Violence in the family reflects a misunderstanding of the identity of androgynes who try to change their appearance from male to female. They have to face pressure from their families who may refuse to accept their new identities. Without acceptance, they may have to leave their families to reduce conflict, or to avoid verbal or physical violence from the family, which may try to force them into behavioral or appearance changes to comply with the birth gender. Parents will explain that these things are done with good intentions and love because they know other people will insult and gossip about their hermaphrodite or 'ladyboy' children; in fact, most of their reasons are concerned with the community or people outside the family, and the social standing of the family in the community. They try to change their children instead of creating an understanding within the community. In some families, where the only son is a hermaphrodite, the son will have to face even more pressure, both from the family and society, because of the expectation for him to continue the family name, to take care of the family, and to be the patriarch of the family.

The last two points have been contested by many hermaphrodites or androgynes, who have proven that they can take care of and lead a family, and some argue against the ideology that continuing the family name depends on the male, saying that they too can continue the family name, but not the lineage; they can earn merit and respect for the family name, but they will not have children to continue the lineage; therefore, continuing the family name doesn't mean continuing the lineage.

The pressure from the family usually comes from the father, who is the leader of the family, and having a hermaphrodite son is interpreted to mean that the father has failed in raising his child. Because of his love, the concern for his own image and family image, he tries to change these things without complete knowledge of the situation. Parents usually think that, because these are 'their' children, they have the right to manage their lives while forgetting that their children are also human with their own bodies and minds that can feel pain, sadness, and disappointment. Violence is thus justified by the reason that parents must take care of their children, and can punish their children when they behave badly.

However, the perception that being an androgyne is something unusual, unnatural, even immoral is all wrong. Society gives the superior status to the parents, enabling them to act upon their children to 'right the wrong' with a cultural violence that invokes parents' responsibility to their children, without any consideration to the method or how their children are turned into the victim of violence in the family. Such violence in families has accumulated for a long time. Parents who have come to terms with the issue will usually say things such as 'he is our child, whether he is good or bad, he's still our child' or 'he can be whatever he wants as long as he is also a good person', and many other things. However, in these cases, the acceptance of these sexually different children is not really the acceptance of their identity, but the acceptance of another status, the status of a child, while their sexuality is effectively overlooked. This is a psychological mechanism of the parents to accept new sexuality of their child, or otherwise it could turn into deep-rooted violence in the mind. We can see that patriarchy is working in silence to influence the beliefs of people in the society regarding paradigms of fatherhood, manliness, family leadership, and manhood. Anyone who attempts to walk out of the old conception will be slapped back into compliance, without concern for the fact that the slap itself is a form of violence and abuse.

Obviously, sex, sexuality and gender cannot possibly be separated; they are in fact significantly linked. According to the book *Gender and the Politics of History*, written by Joan Scott (1982, p. 2), gender status is the social organization of the differences between sexes. However, this does not mean that gender status reflects or implies absolute meanings; nor is it grounded in natural physical differentiation between the male and the female. Instead, gender status refers to the ways in which we establish the meaning of physical differentiation. Thus, gender status is not static and will change according to social, cultural, political and economic contexts. Gender status is bound up in the worth, value, attitude, thinking, belief and practices of human beings in individual societies. Moreover, these individual human responses may be dominated by cultures, politics, economic systems (such as capitalism), globalization, conservative customs and male or female influences, et cetera. These may affect whether or not other gender statuses can be openly performed.

Language further extends the value differences between men and women in the ideology era with phrases such as, 'a woman is a buffalo, while a man is a human being' or 'a woman is rice, while a man is paddy' or 'a man is the elephant's forelegs (leader), while a woman is the hind legs (follower)'. All these proverbs can create values that support a patriarchal system. This patriarchal system—a system on behalf of men as a social group— is created or established in order that men play a higher and more powerful role than women (O'Brien, 1981).

As a matter of fact, it can be considered a sign of weakness in men that they try to aggrandize their own position as a counter to the reproductive role of women, who play the more essential parts in pregnancy and child rearing. Some feminist analysts say that anxiety over reproduction is at the heart of patriarchy. During sexual intercourse, the power relationship between male and female for negotiation and defeat are also counted as part of the sexual experience.

It can be seen that tools or mechanisms which transfer the powerful relations could be shown in education, culture, religion, politics, law and economy. This address aims to specifically mention the gender status of the group that is rarely mentioned in the main social area: homosexuals, both gay and lesbian. However, these groups have also absorbed patriarchy for use in their life practices or their ways of life.

Gender Status with Sexual Variety and the Search for Identity

Feminism has become a principle of education as well as a good example of learning how to support groups of homosexuals, especially in Thailand, where many activist groups work closely and collaborate with each other to on the subject of gender status in Thai society. They cooperate with women's organizations, and the results of such concerted effort have included changes in laws regarding prefixing women's names (women's title), new laws protecting equality for homosexuals or for those who consider themselves of other gender status, attempts to define identities in society through language and unity, and building safe social spaces for sexual diversity.

Currently, homosexuals in Thai society have become an important and increasingly accepted part of the social community, and they keep improving their status constantly, trying to claim for themselves gender equality, especially for those who are working in the public sector, establishing more networks to support gender and sexual rights, exchanging knowledge with other societies, helping towards a better understanding of employment issues, et cetera. Gatherings of homosexual groups have succeeded in attracting the media and other networks. This is a means of opening more spaces to express the multiple identities of people in different sexual dimensions for the ultimate purpose of garnering understanding. Peter Jackson notes that Thai society in the past expressed fewer differences between the sexes than it has now, such as dress, hairstyles, and the married name adopted by either men or women, who more often than not retained their original name. This does not mean that people in past generations did not know which sex they were. Rather, there were no sex classifications in the realm of work and doing one's duty. However, the definition of sex in the past was unlike that in the present. Most importantly, for homosexuals, they were often mentioned in the past as the third sex. It was difficult to identify or categorize men and women with different sexual orientations.

In the era of globalization, capitalism established firm roots, particularly during the colonial period. As that process took hold in Thailand, clothes became distinctly male and female. Work was classified as work for men and for women. However, today, while the differentiating characteristics of women and men are obvious and visible, the classification of gender is still unclear. For example, men who dress like women are sometimes called Metro Sexual men. This group doesn't define itself as as homosexual group. With an unclear status, it can jump forward into either side or just jump out of the frame, outside the classifications of men and women. The status of becoming or being can be confusing to a society that does not understand the status of sexuality. Those people may always feel frustrated, offended, denied and objected to. Therefore, a process of building understanding in the public about the changes of gender, emotions and behavior was then embarked upon.

Sex Variety and Sexual Discriminations

A revision of the laws of the land to endorse the legal rights of different gender statuses is not enough to ensure acceptance in society or to create positive change in the lives of the sexually diverse, because Society does not exist only the basis of legality; there are several other factors as well. However, since Thai society still relies upon government power to control peace, order, and justice, through regulations or policies that people in the country have to follow, changes in the law are a necessary tool of social negotiation, as well as a social symbol. Therefore, we require a movement to modify the laws, perhaps through gender variety networks that try to find opportunities to work with the public sector and the society at large in order to design laws and regulations to end discrimination.

The Constitution of the Kingdom of Thailand BE 2550, Section 30, says: 'All persons are equal before the law and shall enjoy protection under the law. Men and women shall enjoy equal rights. Unjust discrimination against a person on the grounds of the difference in orgin, race, language, sex, age, disability, physical or heath condition, personal status, economic or social standing, religious belief, education or constitutionally political view shall not be permitted.' Prior to the enactment of the constitution Section 30, there was an attempt to use the words 'Sexual Diversity or gender or sexuality' in this section; this effort was network driven by organizations and certain senators, but it was not successful. Nevertheless, the issue of gender was interpreted and included in the appendix to explain the ideas of sexual diversity, sexual identity, and sexuality, in order to clarify that gender is not limited to the distinctions between men and women. This made the law extend itself to provide protections that were not its main purview. In spite of these measures, sex discrimination within the law is an obvious fact. Androgyne applicants have been reported as abnormal, mentally ill or maniacal in the military conscription process; scholarly groups and other networks have called for an end to such discriminatory conscription reports. Furthermore, there is a Red Cross regulation which does not allow the acceptance of blood donations from male homosexuals for the reason that these groups may have higher rates of HIV infection or AIDS risk. Officials try to use so-called 'medical knowledge' to explain this ruling as being right. There is also a movement to ban homosexuality in some entertainment places and hotels in Pattaya. Meanwhile, gays are banned from sitting in Krathong Base during the Krathong festival in Chiang Mai; this group has demanded in the Administrative Court that their rights be considered in the matter.

Recently, there was a debate regarding the appropriateness of the film titled *Insects in the Backyard*, directed by a gay man and dealing with sexual themes and emphasizing the family problems that exist in an actual society. Ultimately, the state used its power to restrict artistic freedoms, arguing that the film was contrary to the good morals of the people. The Ministry of Culture subsequently disseminated statements to the media about why rating classification should be used to disallow certain films being shown. The reasons connected to this particular film were that there was a sex scene between bisexual men in which some of their sex organs were shown, there was a scene between a male student and a female student in uniform having sex; and, lastly, there was a scene where a child dreamed about killing his father. The government's reaction to sex in that film showed that there are many types of social discrimination in play. In contrast, the government made no effort to ban films with explicit heterosexual scenes designed to sexually arouse viewers.

These discriminatory actions are embedded in bias and prejudice, and, ironically, even as they moralize, they are as violations of a moral system. Although the Constitution says in Section 4 'human dignity, equality, liberty and the rights of a person shall be protected', in reality, whatever that person is, she or he is still obligated to function in this society, and is thus compelled by the same society to conform.

Creating Space in Seizing the Chance to Give New Meaning to the Existence of the Homosexuals

Space to express the human dignity of this group in Thai society is over a decade old, and extends to spheres of entertainment, academia, and culture, involving social law and regulation as they adapt to the changes among the sexually diverse, as well as changes in society. The government should create opportunities for learning, integration, cooperation and creating new ideas. Topics in sex education should not be limited to male and female genders, reproductive methods and sexually transmitted diseases. Other topics, such as sexuality, other genders, relationships, and emotion management, should be included. Social campaign agendas, also, should be broadened; not only should they cover subjects such as preserving virginity, fidelity, premarital sex prevention, dealing with many sexual partners, but also to more open ones. These campaigns should provide useful guidelines to help people coping with values conflicts in areas such as monogamy and pre-marital sex. All involved parties should encourage more liberating choices and avoid double standards. And this is only a part of contributing to new understandings in society.

Heterosexuality and Culture of Gender

Ideologies which control sexual practices are deeply rooted in social institutions but are often overlooked. The belief that sexuality is taboo should be eliminated to encourage positive and productive learning. In Thai society, sexuality remains taboo; homosexuality is completely unacceptable. The question is, within a patriarchal society, how can we have a culture that allows positive and productive sexual learning? How can such culture be free from the government's interference? How can it preserve human values from social biases?

Movement of Powerful Ideas

To change social acceptance and provide access to space, we require adjustments in the spheres of law, culture, human rights, sexual rights and access to information. Attitude adjustment in gender issues and diversity is not easily possible. However, its possibility can increase by effective strategies—encouraging people's participation, promoting advocacy, linking community with society, strengthening the homosexual community in all dimensions, spreading unbiased information, seeking support from social and political partners and creating groups to support gender diversity. Our bias can obstruct these strategies. Thus, we should eliminate ignorance, misconception, ideologies and bias.

References

O'Brien, Mary. *The Politics of Reproduction.* London : Routedge and Kegan Paul, 1981.

Scott, Joan Wallach. *Gender and the Politics of History.* New York : Columbia University Press, 1988.

Panel I: Gender and Patriarchy

Seema Luitel

Nepal was caught in sociopolitical violence for over a decade due to armed conflict or the People's War launched by the Communist Party of Nepal (Maoists) in February 1996. The armed conflict had deep but varying impacts on development and on all social groups. The poor and excluded people, especially women, members of the dalit caste, disadvantaged indigenous people and marginalized groups, became the worst victims of the conflict and their precarious position with respect to livelihood became severely affected. As a result, many of them had to leave their homes and live their lives as internally displaced persons (IDPs). A large proportion of the IDPs are still unable to return home for fear of reprisal and inadequate social and livelihood security. Moreover, many of them are bereft of much needed support and have to cope with unhealed psychological trauma on their own.

The second People's Movement in April 2006 that ousted the direct royal regime and reinstalled democracy in Nepal, also kick started the peace process in Nepal because it uniquely brought together the conflicting parties as a pro-democratic force against the autocratic rule. Currently, the country is in a post-conflict transitional period of rehabilitation, reconciliation and reconstruction of a society that has endured centuries of discrimination and inequality. Despite unprecedented political changes,[1] poverty, injustice and poor governance still persist.

The People's Movement, together with the decade long People's War, has undoubtedly brought some positive changes, such as increased representation of women and excluded groups in the Constituent Assembly, which has got the mandate to write a new constitution for Nepal. We can attribute the current increased empowerment of women to the People's War which mobilized and emancipated women from their stereotypical gender roles in society.

Patriarchal as well as feudal structures prevalent in the Nepalese society have placed women in a discriminated position regardless of class, caste, ethnicity, religion and age. Among the 31 percent of Nepalese who fall below the poverty line, the impact of poverty is more severe on women and girls.

The Constituent Assembly, with 197 women members, which is about 32.7% of the total members, has brought a historical change in the representation of women in the legislative structure of Nepal. However, as only a few of these women are in the decision making positions in their respective political parties, their voice and agency do not find adequate space in the decision making structure of political parties.

Thus, issues related to women's rights are often diluted by political leadership dominated by men. The interim constitution has also declared 33 percent representation of women in state machinery at all levels. Nevertheless, a mechanism for proper implementation of this provision is yet to be developed.

Gender is an integral part of all social, political, economic and religious systems and often central to those systems. As a result, it is always challenging to unmask the issues, initiate to intervene and raise the voice against structured domination since these are all protected by the strong patriarchal and feudal system in the Nepalese context.

Human rights instruments, relevant to gender based discrimination and exclusion, include the UNDRIP, Convention on the Rights of the Child (CRC), the Geneva Conventions, Convention on Elimination of All forms of Discrimination Against Women, UNSC Resolution 1325/1820/1612 and 1888.

Development Programmes in the Peace Process

Recently, quite a significant number of development organizations and the government itself are becoming involved in the reconciliation and peace process—post conflict programmes have mushroomed since 2006. These development organizations are mainly responding to the new emerging conflicts, providing necessary support to disqualified Maoist combatants, implementing development programmes, awareness, advocacy, campaigns and media mobilization and many more.

'Peace Building from Below'

The project of building peace at the grassroots level requires common ground, as an entry point to address the structural causes:

- Understanding and definiting of peace at grassroots level
- Working in partnership with community based organizations

Strategic Intervention

Strategic inverventions must begin with these efforts:

- Implementation of gender strategy
- Setting parameters for organizational assessment
- Demand based training based on organizational assessment (Peace and Conflict Management and Gender Equality and Social Inclusion)
- Integration of gender component
- Psychosocial counseling
- Introduction of PCIA tool
- Different approach to refer target groups (CAP, disadvantage, Poor and Excluded, Women, Children, Youth)

Progress towards Results

Some major changes observed thus far are as follows:

- Some dalit caste-focused CBOs have changed their names and now include all non-dalits among the CBPOs members
- Many CBOs have appointed women as a executive committee members
- Men have made a commitment towards supporting women and not tolerating gender based violence.

In spite of progress, still there is a huge gap in advocacy, and a persistent reluctance to participate. Therefore, constant advocacy from the central to local level is must. These efforts must account for a gap in micro and macro level linkages, which has resulted in a failure to capture documentary information and narratives of promising practices. Finally, we must all work toward an awareness and clarity that gender is a matter of great importance for both men and women.

Notes

1. This, among others, includes the election to the Constituent Assembly and the end of the 240 year old monarchy with the formal declaration of Nepal as a federal democratic republic on 28 May 2008 by the first meeting of the Constituent Assembly (CA).

Panel II: Politics, Nation-States and Militarism

Padmamalini Rao

As the ad-hoc spokesperson of the Politics, Militarism and Nation States panel, I wish to introduce myself as we begin this second session: I had come here as a participant—much as we all begin life itself. As a child I journeyed from my Indian origins to the USA. I had struggled with identity ... my Western conceptions packaged in Hindu beliefs. I had travelled over many years from Brazil to China, Singapore, Japan and India as a woman in the gender-challenged world of business, only to return to India to a life of home, hearth and family, steeped in the traditions of my ancestors. More recently, I have adopted the role of a teacher and editor, tools I thought were implements of emancipation—financial independence, influence over young minds and thus the future inheritors of our earth, perhaps the last stronghold of idealism in a world of continuous bargain and barter. The bottom line is that I was, am and always will be a female participant in the greatest modern experiment of perpetual displacement.

As I sit in the first session of this panel, the pieces of my identity, my very self, stand out in perfect relief, each part a component of a whole and yet whole in itself. I shared that I, too, was a sovereign entity at war with myself, both victim and perpetrator of the politics of choice and survival, and of authority both received and doled out. In my five foot three inch persona, I am no different from a Thailand at civil war, grappling with its diverse parts, its ancient heritage, its modern garb, its politics of existence, its need as a nation state to rule and exert authority and be ruled by its parts, its citizens.

I am not a scholar. I have no works of my own to cite. My beliefs, my convictions are my faith. So, the text I rely upon for my participation in this Congress was a 2010 Peace Proposal, titled 'Towards a New Era of Value Creation', written by my mentor, Dr Daisaku Ikeda, President of Soka Gakkai International, a lay Buddhist organization recognized by the United Nations for promoting peace, culture and education through the philosophy of the Buddha's *Lotus Sutra* as expounded by the fourteenth century Japanese saint, Nichiren Daishonin. The central philosophy of the *Lotus Sutra* is that universal peace is achieved when each one of us achieves individual peace, that true enlightenment is working for the happiness of oneself AND others, that the highest 'cause' one can create to achieve the 'effect' of enlightenment is the awakening of compassion, pure acceptance as they are, for another, the 'other'. Dr Ikeda has submitted a peace proposal to the United Nations every year since 26 January 1983. This, the 28th peace proposal, is a blue print for the most effective way of achieving a peaceful world: through 'soft power'. Dr Ikeda is a recipient of over 310 honorary doctorates from universities all over the world including the University of California, Los Angeles (UCLA), Moscow State University, Beijing Normal University, University of Buenos Aires, University of Macau, University of the Philippines, Harvard University, Chinese University of Hong Kong, Gandhi Smriti and Darshan Samiti, Chinese Academy of Social Sciences, University of Bologna, Ateneo de Santander, Rajiv Gandhi Institute for Contemporary Studies amongst others.

The Thai delegates have expressed their deep anguish about the recent civil disturbances in Thailand, where the Thai military, young men, soldiers, have been forced into aggression against their own fellow Thais of the southern provinces. Participants have expressed their shock at the extant of discrimination one Thai was capable of inflicting upon another. Suddenly, the southern Thai has become the 'other', compounded further by the fact that the Thai military consists of both southerners and northerners. I quote Dr Ikeda:

> Ortega y Gasset considered our willingness and capacity to coexist peacefully with those who are different from us as that which divides barbarity and civilization.

> In my dialogue with former Soviet President Mikhail Gorbachev, the man who dramatically restored debate and dialogue to the political culture of the Soviet Union, we concurred on the importance of learning to respect others, accustoming and accommodating ourselves to the reality of otherness. I ... defined nihilism as a refusal to feel the moral sense of value that compels us to engage with people as unique and irreplaceable individuals.

It is not easy to replace physical violence with words and dialogue. We are discussing how dialogue is possible when the speakers acknowledge each other as worthy to be spoken to. So even before words can replace violence, 'the reality of otherness' must be accommodated. Obviously, a shift in thinking is necessary. I ask you, 'How can we make it possible to look beyond the masks of North versus South, Thai military versus civilian?' Can we as individuals see the 'man' behind the uniform and recognize that he was someone's son, brother, much like anyone of us? Can we 'accustom' ourselves with the possibility that no matter how brutal he was, he must have expressed tenderness to someone somewhere in his young life? Can we hang on to this sliver of a capacity for compassion and build trust, break barriers and utter words?

Ana, a doctor working on the Thai-Myanmar border in refugee camps, talks during our first session about the brutalities she has seen committed by torturers and experienced by hapless victims: she has lost faith in humanity and has come to the World Peace Congress desperate to understand this strange word we call 'peace' and whether there is any realistic hope in achieving peace in this world ever. She speaks of her experience trying to reconstruct human bodies subjected to unspeakable violation and the complete lack of remorse in the eyes of the perpetrators.

Nichiren Buddhism tells us that good exists with evil and that our role is to do our best every day to overcome that evil. I quote Dr Ikeda: 'No matter how great the divide between our ideals and reality may be, there is no need to give up hope or accept this with resignation. Instead, the ordinary citizens of the world need to come together to create a new reality.' My mentor says that that a 'new reality' has to be 'jointly promoted by individuals, organizations, spiritual and religious groups, universities and research institutions, as well as agencies within the UN system.' I quote my mentor's own mentor, Josei Toda: 'There is no easy path to the realization of good ...' but we must know that the solutions lie at the level of the individual. Ordinary people must empower themselves, their families and communities to resist oppression with dialogue, humanity and compassion.

During our first session, I suggest that communities must take the initiative to reach out to military personnel camped there by using the community's local institutions such as schools, women's groups, community centres etc. Soldiers could be encouraged to interact with people on weekends in their civilians' clothing, shedding their uniform. Both sides could be encouraged to see each other's human face. I expected guffaws. I look around wondering if someone is going to snigger, 'Lady, were you born yesterday?' Dr Ikeda quotes Paul Valery, saying '"Words like virtue, nobility, honour, honesty, generosity, have become almost impossible to use or else they have acquired bastard meanings; language is no longer equipped for legitimately praising a man's character"', which Simone Weil further qualifies as 'the enfeeblement of the sense of value'. But I am representing a movement 'to dispel the clouds of nihilism in order to reveal the language and values of good that languish on the verge of extinction ... to revive the human spirit and reawaken ordinary citizens, ...' so it is no surprise that no one scoffs. No one criticized this suggestion as being hopelessly idealistic. On the contrary, everyone takes to the idea of empowerment of the community. Others have stopped me to say that they felt my words seemed to come from my heart and give them hope.

The reality is that something profound has dawned in me during our first session: the blueprint for peace, the soft power my mentor was talking about is none other than the three-pronged weapon of 'work', 'women' and 'children'. Work can be equated with 'a contributive way of life', in the words of Tsunesaburo Makiguchi, the first president of the Soka Gakkai. It is a way of life that encourages independent living, 'looking out for our own needs' while concerning ourselves with 'the sufferings of others'. In the Peace Proposal, Dr Ikeda 'urge[s] governments to make efforts to address unemployment ... [because] human dignity is gravely threatened when individuals are employed under inhumane or degrading conditions, or if lack of job security makes it impossible to plan realistically for the future'. The first panel discussion reveals a deep sense of the Thai government having neglected the economic security of the southern provinces, making the South deeply discontented and further humiliated by military backlash.

Women, the second prong, are at the heart of society. While all men and women are protagonists in the pursuit of peace, women are the ultimate teachers and, as Dr Ikeda says, 'Empowering a girl through education will lead to a brighter future for herself, her family and her children, eventually permeating society as a whole with the light of hope'. While women could be said to be at the heart of society, schools and universities could be considered the heart of a community. Together, here is a nursery of humanistic, peace promoting individuals for all of society. Central to Dr Ikeda's Peace Proposal is the fact that he invites women (teachers) and students to create a new paradigm for peace.

Finally, children, the third prong and the main beneficiaries of the '21st century to be a century of peace and coexistence', are to be protected, nurtured and strengthened in the culture of peace:

> The Declaration and Programme of Action on a Culture of Peace, adopted by the General Assembly in 1999, calls all relevant actors to 'Ensure that children, from an early age, benefit from education on the values, attitudes, modes of behavior and ways of life to enable them to resolve any dispute peacefully and in a spirit of respect for human dignity and of tolerance and non-discrimination.'

It is children (and by extrapolation, students) who ensure that, in the words of Arnold J. Toynbee, 'we are not deemed to make history repeat itself; it is open to us, through our own efforts, to give history ... some new and unprecedented turn'. And as such, the Soka Gakkai has 'continued to urge that the happiness of children be the standard for measuring the success of any effort to resolve the problems confronting society'.

On the second day, we are asked to put these discussions and ideas into the form of a resolution that can be passed. Inexplicably, I have been assigned two students (children to me) to assist us. The background canvas of the resolution we are crafting is that the military, army, and politicians are none other than people from our own communities who were once children themselves. The institutional face of politics and state and military must be replaced by the human face. Dr. Daisaku Ikeda, third founding president of Soka Gakkai International says, 'No matter how great the divide between our ideals and reality may be, there is no need to give up hope or accept this. Instead, the ordinary citizens of the world need to come together to create a new reality. The prohibitions on land mines and cluster weapons that have been realized in recent years are the fruit of such solidarity.' The heart of the resolution must be to use schools and women of the community to initiate dialogue with military units in the community. During our first session, I stated that the backbone of the resolution should be Dr Ikeda's tools of dialogue, trust in the other person's inherent good, return to our common humanity and unconditional respect for all individuals, friendship and including diversity into a unity.

Just as I am wondering whether any of this will make sense, a young student stands up to support my suggestion, saying that there is already an innovative programme, started by a Thai military officer, where one soldier and one university student from Mahidol University live in pairs in a camp, sharing a room and interacting with each other on a daily basis. The leader of this interactive programme is always a woman chosen from the university, and her deputy is always a man from the military.

Unexpectedly, a powerful example has emerged from the co-respective and co-operative process that brings me and this Congress panel and our participants together. And oh what an example! Here at the center of it is a woman and students (children). In Buddhism, actual proof, or in modern parlance, 'the proof of the pudding' being in the eating of it, is far superior to theoretical proof. So, while I have not been party to the grassroots project of Mahidol University to promote peace, I had foretold it in our first panel session (not by the genius of my mind but by the logic of Dr Ikeda's blueprint for peace); and in this second session, I have mystically become a part of its retelling, its affirmation of its own validity and, therefore, its perpetuity.

The pieces of my identity have settled, one fitting with the other, and I am happy as I have never been, an essential state of being if we want to contribute anything at all towards the larger achievement of peace.

Dr. Ikeda writes: 'It is imperative that we always resist the temptation to abandon dialogue and adopt violence in its place. We must remain committed to the process of philosophical hesitation, enduring tension and the smelting furnace of ceaseless spiritual struggle; for this is the one place where our humanity can be truly forged.' Dr Ikeda says we must be 'proactive, self-reliant agents of change, transforming the era', and it is this thought that makes me hope that this Congress harbingers an era where every minute there is a Congress of dialogue for peace happening somewhere, whether between the four walls of a family home or the larger stage of human drama.

Reference

2010 Peace Proposal - Daisaku Ikeda http://www.daisakuikeda.org/assets/files/peace2010.pdf

Panel III - Religion, Morality, and Transcendent Ethics

Ritu Datta

Peace has to be more than a slogan, hope or idea and has to acquire the dynamism of moral and spiritual action.

We need to spread awareness about this simple fact: just as we have reached this venue from various parts of the globe for this one purpose, similarly, to evolve as human beings or to be one with the divine we follow different philosophies and religions for one purpose. If I am a *true* Hindu, then understanding and respecting other religions should not be a problem. In fact, this acceptance will be a sign of an open-minded individual, reflecting the conditions for peace within ourselves and in our environments, too.

As Gandhi-*ji* said, '*be the change you want to see in the world*' so let's start from the 'self'. If each one of us is at peace within, the world will improve.

This reminds me of another one of Gandhi-ji's mantras about the power of 'thought'. When a particular thought is contemplated long enough, with concentration and with feelings of goodwill, it produces strong vibrations in the atmosphere. Even science has proved that radio waves and thought waves travel at the same speed.

Our freedom movement in India is a good example of how Gandhi-ji, with his paradigm of the power of thought, could invoke patriotic fervor in every Indian; and the result was our country's freedom.

We all have experienced the power of thought sometime in life. I would like to ask all of us to give more 'thought' to the power of peace rather than to negative forces.

Most of the time, peace is disturbed by 'anger' ... Anger is an important emotion, one that needs to be tamed. One incident or accident can create havoc. I would like to give an example from my film on the same subject, *We Do*, which works with the metaphor that a matchstick has a head but no brains; hence it flares up with little friction, and then passes that ignition on to others. By contrast, as human beings, 'We Do' have brains ... so we should not flare up so easily. The film opens with a Kathakali dancer whose expression changes to anger; the word DANGER transforms to ANGER, and a matchstick is lit, which in turn burns all the matchsticks in the box. Film clips, juxtaposed with the Kathakali dancer, project this friction. Finally, from the flames emerge these words: *The humble matchstick has a head but no brains*. The film ends with the words, *WE DO*.

Hypothetically, if we say 80% of the world population wants peace, then only 20% is against it; so if we, the majority, put our strong belief and the power of 'thought' into 'peace' ... we will soon succeed. The idea is so simple, yet, at the same time, it is demanding because it involves changing our approach to life. Such is the price we have to pay for peace—but, at that price, it is an absolute bargain.

*Film stills from *We Do*. 2008. Ritu Datta, Director.*

But no brains...

Panel III: Religion, Morality, and Transcendent Ethics

Karen Ohnesorge

Our agenda today has four parts, which panelists will begin to address with opening statements, and which we hope to explore more fully in collaboration with our audience. First, we wish to very briefly describe the philosophies that govern us, and their relationship to our assigned Resolutions, originally drafted at the 2007 World Peace Congress. Second, we will share past experiences from some of our projects related to peace, whether we met with success or obstacles, in order to lend wise council to one another. Third, we will establish our criteria for a good proposal, to respond to our charge for the present Congress. And, finally, we will craft a practical action proposal that meets our criteria, that draws on our rich experiences, and that is aligned with our own philosophies as well as with our Resolutions. The synergy of panel and audience will help us create a clear and effective proposal, which we can then 'offer to people and nations in conflict'.

To begin our conversation, I will quickly outline my own philosophy or ethic, which lies at the crossroads of two ideals: human reciprocity and generative imagination.

I define human reciprocity as the primal, natural process of exchange among people. I certainly concede that this process can be corrupted by ego, capitalism, sexism, racism, or nationalism; however, at its foundation, human reciprocity is a real and blessed consequence of the fact that we share space on this planet, at this national border, in this room, in these bodies. In this (ideal) process of exchange, human beings speak and act without fear of reprisal, and they hear and receive understanding from one another, without presumptions (which often arise from self-interest) or denials (which may emerge based on perceived threats).

Two proponents of human reciprocity are Enrique Dussel (1934-) and Paulo Freire (1921–1997). Dussel, an Argentinian ethicist who is now a citizen of Mexico, is one of the founders of liberation philosophy. He subscribes to the optimistic notion that one being's cry of distress obligates ('interpellates') the hearer to take action on behalf of the person who is suffering. For Dussel, the value of human existence is to be found, for all people, in our response to this innate and universal capacity to experience empathy. Dussel says, furthermore, that the motivation and impulse to act on behalf of a fellow being emerges from the 'immediate corporeality', or physical nearness to one another, of the hearer and the sufferer (22). We must practice love for our neighbor, simply because our neighbor has called out to us.

Like Dussel, we may wish to 'propose a Philosophy of Liberation of the Other that is beyond the horizon of the economic-political-hegemonic world (fratricide), of the Eurocentric communication community (filicide), of the phallic eroticism which castrates women (uxoricide) and last but not least, the subject which uses nature as an exploitable mediation for the valorization of the value of capital (ecocide)' (20-21). This Philosophy of Liberation would seek to operate independent of the major forces of indoctrination and domination that fuel violence and refute peace. As Dussel declared, 'if there is an Absolute, it cannot but affirm and develop the person in justice, autonomy, and freedom'(11); in other words, an ethic that transcends violence and attains to peace makes its final appeal to an Absolute, whether postulated as a philosophical construct or known through mystical experiences.

Others have shared Dussel's dedication to human reciprocity, and a particular influence on Dussel's work was educator and philosopher Paulo Freire. Freire practiced what is called 'liberation pedagogy'," or the *Pedagogy of the Oppressed*; he believed that 'radical love' is fundamental to teaching and learning. Both devoutly Catholic and thoroughly Marxist, Freire presented radical love as deep compassion and open-hearted curiosity—in other words, a process of human reciprocity. He expressed this radical love as an educator through a teaching philosophy that eschewed dictatorial practices such as lectures and recitations. He felt these traditional methods were merely a way to make submission into a habit for all learners; to counter these practices, he designed a method that empowered learners. And his work had compelling results: during his initial experiment in literacy education in 1962, he was able to teach 300 non-literate adults in the city of Recife, Brazil how to read within the space of forty-five days. In fact, his pedagogy was so effective in bringing literacy to the people that he was exiled from Brazil for about fifteen years, since his work resulted in newly qualified voters who threatened to destabilize government control of elections.

Described very briefly, Freire's method was to bring a group of teachers to a community, and to live there among the people, sharing their work, their food, and their culture. In this way, Freire established mutual understanding and trust. Once embedded in the community, artists and photographers among the teachers would begin gathering images of ordinary local life. At sessions involving community groups, Freire would bring a photograph or drawing to the table and ask, 'what do you see?' The answers to that question became the core vocabulary for the coming weeks, when those gathered would then assemble the practical realities of daily life to form sentences, paragraphs, and arguments. The rocks and earth of experience became the foundation for the curriculum. In that question—*what do you see?*—is a world of curiosity and compassion, one that nurtures authentic selves who are agents of positive change.

This human reciprocity may find its fullest expression when it intersects with generative imagination. For its part, human reciprocity fosters a peaceful environment—an ethical realm—in which human agents can operate. Generative imagination contributes an energetic wellspring for action; it is a force that, for me, arises from my meditative practices as a poet and artist. In short, generative imagination is the notion that our very creativity forms our experiences, relationships, and material realities in the most transformative (or totalizing) ways—for good (or ill). So language is important; image is important; sound is important. As ethical beings we are thus called ('interpellated') to be responsible in how we represent the world and evoke the senses of others. And in exercising our generative imagination, we require Grace, as a construct that honestly regards our limitations, while also inviting miracles—in order to work for Peace.

This two-part philosophy or ethic shapes my approach to our Resolutions. I am seeking:

- To be true to myself, and to provide conditions that encourage others to do the same, with human reciprocity as a touchstone. Others at this Congress have called this reciprocity 'deep listening'.
- To practice respect for all faiths and to honor diversity through this spirit of human reciprocity.
- To encourage realization of individual spirituality and collective service to humanity, calling upon our shared generative imagination—the gift of creativity—to sustain our dedication to action.

We have promised to talk briefly about our past and current peace projects. Much of my career has been devoted to making higher education accessible to all people, regardless of race, class, disability, or gender. This work has taken place in grant-funded projects, U.S. Federal TRIO Programs set up to assist students with low incomes or disabilities, as well as those who are in the first generation of their families to attend college. I have also been involved in helping to encourage spiritual growth as part of the life of U.S. college students. I currently serve as the Dean of Instruction for the College of Ottawa University, a U.S. institution that is affiliated with the American Baptist Church (the Christian denomination that ordained Dr Martin Luther King, Jr.), and that was established in 1865 by an agreement between the Baptists and the Native American Ottawa Tribe (with whom we have re-established strong ties). One element of our mission is to be a 'Christ-centered community of Grace'; another unstated element of our mission is to 'serve the underserved'. Finally, as a professor of English, I have also worked with students at all levels to understand how autobiography can be a self-unifying document, an opportunity to understand one's process of internal growth, and to unfold a profoundly spiritual life. Future peace-related projects include serving as one of a few host institutions for the Rutgers Leadership Institute, which encourages women to engage in politics through service projects.

Our work for universal harmony, today and in the coming weeks, will present tremendous challenges. For poet Wislawa Szymborska, writing a poem entitled 'Torture', the conditions of suffering are relentless: 'the body is and is and is' (47). However, as Venerable Bikkhuni Dhammananda reminds us, Buddhism teaches that only with this body can we be enlightened. Our purpose in this panel session is to come together for an embodied and reciprocal dialogue about spirituality and ethics, and thereby to imagine a path toward peace for our planet.

References

Dussel, Enrique. *The Underside of Modernity: Apel, Ricoeur, Rorty, Taylor, and the Philosophy of Liberation.* Translated and Edited by Eduardo Mendieta. Atlantic Highlands, NJ: Humanities P International, 1996.

Freire, Paulo. *Pedagogy of the Oppressed.* Translated by Myra Bergman Ramos. New York: Continuum, 1993.

Szymborska, Wislawa. *Miracle Fair: Selected Poems of Wislawa Szymborska.* Translated by Joanna Trzeciak. New York: Norton, 2002.

Panel IV: Law, Human Welfare, Children and Other Species

G. Venkatesh Rao

Introduction

Law is the code that regulates the functioning of a system of governance in any nation. Law therefore can be an instrument of social change for the better or worse, but it ordinarily reflects the philosophy of the nation, its people and government.

Law comprises those sets of rules and guidelines by which a nation, its social, economic and political systems function. Essentially, progress of mankind in every nook and corner of the world has been towards a technologically superior, more sophisticated and efficient political, economic and social system—generally for the welfare and benefit of the people of that society and nation. Therefore, when we look at laws, some of which are static and many of which are dynamic, they are indicators of the mind-set and thinking of the people of those societies and nations, and, as such, endeavor to bring about a transformation in the working of the system. The ultimate goal therefore of governments and laws is human welfare. In modern day parlance, human welfare and social welfare are synonymous and relate to the development of the human being as a member of society

The International Initiative in Human and Social Welfare

When we speak of law, we mean both domestic laws in individual states and nations as well as international law and international organizations promoting social welfare and rights of children and other species. In the last few decades, social welfare has been high on the agenda of international organizations like the United Nations and other similar bodies which are interested in the promoting of basic human and social welfare rights of the people on the globe.

For over half a century, the International Council on Social Welfare (ICSW) has represented peak organisations in over seventy countries. Thus tens of thousands of civil society organisations have been represented through ICSW at the UN. As an organisation with UN consultative status, ICSW is involved in global discussions concerning issues of social development, social welfare and social justice. The ICSW also interacts and works in close association with all UN Organizations who are in the area of development of Social Welfare.

Most of the human and social welfare initiatives are carried out by UN Organizations like the UNESCO, ECOSOC, UN Commission for Social Development and the UN Research Institute for Social Development (UNRISD).

One of the premier UN organizations which is concentrating on social welfare alone is the United Nations Social Welfare Commission (UNSWC) whose primary focus is on

> *... promoting social, development across the world. It provides substantive support to Governments in developing policy measures and initiatives to promote inclusive 'societies for all', where each individual has rights and responsibilities regardless of economic status (poverty), social status (gender, marital), specific age group (older persons, youth), disability or cultural or religious affiliation. The aim is to ensure that individuals and communities are enabled to participate in society and contribute to national development while enjoying basic human rights and fundamental freedoms.*

Most countries have adopted the UN Organizations resolutions and try to ensure that the necessary domestic Governmental support is given with the required urgency. The Member states are also proactive in the implementation of these programs or give active support to them. Member states have also been adopting suitable legislations in their respective countries in order these social welfare laws get translated into law to be enforced by the various state agencies and also ensure, that they are respected and followed by the citizens and residents of the respective countries.

Another definition of the common good, as the quintessential goal of the state, requires an admission of the individual's basic right in society, which is, namely, the right of everyone to the opportunity to freely shape his life by responsible action, in pursuit of virtue and in accordance with the moral law. The common good, then, is the sum total of the conditions of social life which enable people the more easily and straightforwardly to do so. The object of State sovereignty is the free choice of means for creating these conditions. Others, in particular could be described as namely the freedom for the individual to develop himself or herself to the highest possible apogee and enjoy such other rights for the development of human welfare and pursuit of happiness for one's family.

The most pressing items for the concern and consideration of the governments have been in the areas of education, health, hunger relief, disaster relief, environmental protection, and women and child development etc. And further in order to avoid ecological imbalances, the need for animal welfare and the protection and preservation of flora and fauna of the planet become very essential.

Al Gore, winner of the Nobel Peace Prize, said, 'Two thousand scientists, in a hundred countries, engaged in the most elaborate, well organized scientific collaboration in the history of humankind, have produced long-since a consensus that we will face a string of terrible catastrophes unless we act to prepare ourselves and deal with the underlying causes of global warming.'

Human welfare can only be achieved if the governments are conscious of the most important needs and where they should focus their energies. If we need to focus all the energies and resources of the society and nation, the wasteful and unnecessary expenditures have to be curbed. It is here the whole concept of World Peace becomes important, that when governments realize that the resources of the nation cannot be frittered away in conflict management and purchase of armaments meant for war.

When enormous resources of a nation are devoted towards building up of stockpiles of weapons, strengthening the war machines, creating very large armies and devoting so much of the economic development in these areas, it leaves only a very small portion of the finances to devote towards human welfare.

The role of law is extremely important in diverting a nation's focus from violence, military buildup, increasing the armed forces. It is only when the representatives of the people and the law makers understand the significance of diverting the energies of the nation to human welfare measures that they will they take strong and effective steps in arms reduction and renunciation of large armies.

I would like to highlight the issue in discussion by Amartya Sen: 'It is important to reclaim for humanity the ground that has been taken from it by various arbitrarily narrow formulations of the demands of rationality.' In fact, the United Nations Development Programme (UNDP) was the first to intiate an index to measure the development of human welfare, and called it the Human Development Index (HDI). The origins of the HDI are found in the annual Human Development Reports of the United Nations Development Programme. The Human Development Index (HDI) is a composite statistic used to rank countries by level of 'human development' and separate 'very high human development', 'high human development', 'medium human development' and 'low human development' countries.

The Human Development Index (HDI) is a comparative measure of life expectancy, literacy, education and standards of living for countries worldwide. It is a standard means of measuring well-being, especially child welfare. It is used to distinguish whether the country is a developed, a developing or an under-developed country, and also to measure the impact of economic policies on quality of life. There are also HDI for states, cities, villages, et cetera, by local organizations or companies.

There came a shift in development economics from National Income Accounting to people centered policies, which were enunciated by well known and eminent development economists of the world, who worked on newer conceptual frameworks, to measure human development. The economists who contributed to development economics in a big way are Noble Laureate Amartya Sen, Gustav Ranis, Meghnad Desai, Sudhir Anand, Pual Street and Frances Stewart. The new economic philosophy was to evaluate development not only by economic advances but also by measuring the improvements to human well being.

It is, therefore, very clear that the shift in recent decades has been towards use of the Human Development Index, which is a composite and wholesome measure of the human welfare in society that includes the development and safe-keeping of women, children and the environment.

I would like to conclude by saying that my thoughts, as they have been gathered at this session, are beautifully encapsulated by the words of wisdom of His Holiness the Dalai Lama:

> We must recognize that the suffering of one person or one nation is the suffering of humanity. That the happiness of one person or nation is the happiness of humanity; through violence, you may 'solve' one problem, but you sow the seeds for another; as people alive today, we must consider future generations: a clean environment is a human right like any other. It is therefore part of our responsibility toward others to ensure that the world we pass on is as healthy, if not healthier, than we found it.
>
> The creatures that inhabit this earth—be they human beings or animals—are here to contribute, each in its own particular way, to the beauty and prosperity of the world.

Panel IV – Law, Human Welfare, Children and Other Species

Thanomsing Sukosalo

A group of monks from our organisation has been working with several youth who are studying both within and outside schools, including a number who reside in a juvenile training center where 11-24 year-old children and youth are detained.

'Gee ... Are they crazy monks?...' were the first words we heard from the children at the Juvenile training center, referring to our monk lecturers. One day, after some time had gone by, one of our monks instinctively said, 'I have been ordained as a Buddhist novice several times, yet I do not respect Buddhist monks. I do not understand why I have to follow my Venerable teacher. Why do I have to call my venerable teacher a "venerable teacher"? And why do I have to believe my teacher? However, what I understand is that my "venerable teacher" understands me, although I do not understand him at all.

Buddhist monks are representatives of one of the most important institutions in Thailand. The image of being a Buddhist monk has created a gap between us and our targeted children in both positive and negative ways. For instance, some children are taught to pay respect to monks. The belief is embedded in our native tradition. Other children may have grown up in communities where nearby temples may not be respected. This is reflected their negative attitude towards Buddhist monks. Therefore, we have to show them how friendly we are as friends and not as teachers or as any strangers who just come and command them to do this do that. But we should be their good friends who are ready to learn together with them, exchange our ideas with one another, and most importantly show them our sincerity.

While working with children who have been supposedly called 'trouble children', we have to ask ourselves whether or not they are 'trouble' because they have problems. If we start thinking that it is their problems that make them the way they are, working with the children will be mainly focused on how to solve all of their problems instead of guiding them to solve their own problems. However, if we are not with them any day, [if we do not make the effort to interact with them day after day], how can they [learn to] solve their problems by themselves?

We are always aware of the fact that sometimes we spoil ourselves by enjoying playing games or engaging in activities without thinking or taking any responsibilitys for anyone. We have also once been children who were curious to do and try what our elders forbade us to do. Now, when we consider those same activities, we apply the Dhamma's principle teachings because our foundation is Buddhism. This teaching is Dhamma and what everybody expects to gain from Buddhist monks is also Dhamma because Dhamma is Dhamma.

If we considered this optimistically, the world consists of Dhamma because the definitions of Dhamma are simple nature, Dhamma conduct and Dhamma sermons. Nature is the common reality in our world. Everything is derived from life's lessons. Whether good or bad, our experiences form our our own lessons. If we don't learn from these lessons, the lessons will automatically return to teach us continuously and repeatedly. We then express this learning in 'Dhamma conduct', which means knowing to adjust oneself to our surroundings in order to avoid failures that may cause unhappiness to us by repeating these lessons again. Finally, Dhamma sermons mean teachings or stories told by those who have had experiences and and have overcome an unhappy time in their life. Once we learn how to apply these teachings in our lives, we can be more confident that we won't go the wrong way anymore.

That's why we have to analyze thoroughly every problem. For example, if we prefer to apply the Buddha teaching of Dhamma, we have to make sure which section of Dhamma we are going to apply and how we are going to teach it to the children. Our answer is that we choose the Dhamma section labeled 'being-in-good-company.' Since human beings are social creatures and having good friends is what everybody is seeking, for we do believe that having a good friend is always on the path of goodness.

The most important thing we should regard is that a few days cannot change anyone's mind sustainably. Have you ever known anyone who could remember your name even though you don't know his name? Have you ever been impressed by someone with whom you were not familiar at all, but she treated you as if you were her very important relative? This is what we think is the feeling people are looking for when facing a time in their lives when they need caring....

Our actual work began the second we met with a group of youngsters who had been most frequently 'trained' in several types of training. Some of them could rattle out, from the beginning to the end, what we were going to do. Furthermore, one boy in our program was telling us while helping us move our stuff that he had 'passed all the trainings' which he listed out as Buddhist, Christian, and Islamic courses. He said that many people had come to train them here and that most of the activities engaged in were not obviously different from each other.

He said, 'Next, you will do this, then do that.' He was a 'know it all' type. 'Finally I might be crying and feel appreciated. But it doesn't help us in the long run, ' he added.

His [cynical] statements made us more concerned about what had blocked the children from opening themselves to listen to us. We finally had to use a tool from the Buddha's teaching once again. This tool is called the 'Buddha conducts';they consist of four methods as follows:

1. Verification (*santasana*) means that the children should be taken/led to see for themselves, and they should realize that all penalties resulted from their own actions. Their punishments were not derived from having been forced by anyone at all, but they happened because their hearts were not strong enough. For instance, many teenagers who had drug addictions told us that they could not stop having drugs because they had been addicted for a long time. To stop taking narcotic drugs is a serious change that takes a period of time which is

about a year. When we consulted the rehabilitation officials, they told us that the first step of the rehabilitation process is that the patients may be given some similar 'good' drugs such as diazepam or valium for treatment. This made me wonder why narcotics were defined as 'bad' drugs. This means that those who use the drugs will definitely be addicted to them, and when drug addicts need the drug, they will suffer intensely and will try desperately to get the drugs. I do believe that this method of drug rehabilitation [substituting one drug for another so-called less harmless one] is not an appropriate method. Maybe the person who discovered the drug rehabilitation method may not get addicted to the drug before. Our experiment to stop teenagers from having drugs was simply talking with them in a friendly way. We asked them ... what if they use drugs all the time, and they need more drugs but they don't have any money? What should they do then? Some of these teenagers told us that they might rob someone, steal someone's money, or steal some things to sell, etc. It seemed that there were several illegal activities arising from their minds. When we changed the questions such as ... if they had some money, but there were no drug agencies, there were no drugs in the market, what should they do? The answer from the teenagers was that they would just have to give up. When they were asked whether or not they would suffer terribly, they answered that they would not have any problems. After they answered these questions, they started thinking about why they would not have any problems or suffering if they didn't have drugs. It seemed as if they had begun to realize that some drug addiction symptoms were creations of their minds.

If there was no money but there were drugs, they would try to find some money to buy drugs. However, when there was money but no drugs, they had to make up their minds to accept the situation. This realization made us feel that it might be less difficult to stop taking drugs than we had ever thought before. As a result of asking these types of questions, we found that a number of teenagers could stop taking drugs because they could understand that the drug addiction was only in their minds. If they paid attention to having the intention of quitting them, they would be free.

2. Incitement (*samatapana*) is to inspire someone to set his new

and better goal. From our survey, it was found that most teenagers with whom we were working did not have any goal in their life. They just wished to have some food to eat, time to play and rest when they wanted. Or it would be correct to say that they wanted to do whatever they wanted to do. This might be a dream of many people. However, we think that if human beings prefer to set only this goal, the world would certainly be in trouble because everybody prefers to do things on one's own. Therefore, our group encouraged them to exchange their dreams with us, and we, as monks, shared ours with them. As monks, our monks' dreams must absolutely be chosen as Nirvana or enlightenment. Even though enlightenment is the ultimate goal in Buddhism, it is not too difficult to reach. In general, everybody wishes to be happy; therefore enlightenment is the goal that we would like to persuade everyone to pay more attention to in order to realize this dream of happiness. Though the dream of enlightenment may not be achievable now, as long as we keep it as a goal we can be sure that we won't be willing to settle for anything less and worse.

3. Encouragement (*samut taechana*) means to create trust in someone by listening to him sincerely and intentionally. This means that we will stand by him to encourage him to further fight for his life. He will be motivated to perceive that the he will not be traveling to his goal alone, but he still has many friends to accompany him. Importantly, we are the ones who have the same dream as his and are ready to be his good company along his trip.

4. Gladdening (*supahangsana*) means that while travelling, we should be filled with delight and joy. For this part, we chose activities which were appropriate for the youth whose age allowed them to use their vigour. Some activities were exhausting and some relaxing. We ended our activities with storytelling because this is a way they can use their own stories to encourage the others.

All of this has taught us that learning is a two way communication where a teacher could be a learner, and sometimes a learner could be a teacher as well. These activities have created a friendly atmosphere as well, because most people do not like to be taught (but they like teaching people). Training will have been like playing games and doing activities together, but we have to ensure that we have enough time to let the players speak and talk freely. Who knows how chatting comfortably without any tension for a few days may change someone's life? More importantly, it is not that we try to change these youth, but that they try to change themselves.

Then one day the phone rang, and a voice from the other end of the line said, 'Can I come to see you?' From that moment onwards, we realized and continue to realize that one drop of Dhamma was absorbed inside his rigid heart.

And that is when peace making starts.

Panel V: Arts, Culture, Media and Communication

Sornchai Chatwiriyachai

As we begin this second session of the Panel on Arts, Culture, Media and Communication, we must recall how we proceeded through yesterday's session. The Resolutions we write are shaped by our experiences during that gathering.

'Everyone! ... please close your eyes, relax and observe your sitting posture. Try to perceive deeply where we place our right hand and our left hand.' The voice of Master Prasart Pratesrut floated sonorously through the half-new and half-old acoustic system speaker in this luxurious resort in Nakhonnayok Province. I stood woodenly behind the plaited sun screen, acknowledging that I had to be the one to 'create a relaxed atmosphere'. But the electrical control panel at the back of the class was not for the faint of heart. It was professionally installed with lots of switches and dimmers. The electrician in charge must have gone out to have a cigarette somewhere, leaving me with the light controls. It was as if I was a child who, having never even seen a piano before, somehow had landed in front of a grand piano, in a concert hall with a large audience waiting expectantly for something to happen.

I had no other choice but to go with my instincts. It was like shooting in the dark. Some bulbs were too bright, but it would be too dark if they were to be turned off. The minute of hesitant dilemma slowly passing by felt like ages. Master Prasart rang a Japanese bell to lead everyone to a posture of self-control.

A quick glance and I noticed people in the room were from various backgrounds. A group of youngsters, aged between the late 20s to early 30s, studying for Master degrees in Contemplative Education, were from Mahidol University. They were smart, polite and self-controlled. Meena (Geeratigarn Techawattanagool) and the Rainbow Dream Group were present, calling themselves the 'Incredible Females of Lanna Group.' They had been working to increase awareness on the issue of gender in Chiengmai. She was fair and radiant with a native cloth covering her shoulders, like an angel's wing ready to spread and fly for freedom. To the side, one could see a woman of experienced age in an indigo dyed northern Thai style shirt from Petchaburi province, Thailand. She was the representative of a minority group. An elder 'aunty, ' she was chubby but looked strong with burnt brown skin. Her eyes shone with liveliness. She confessed later that she entered the wrong room, but something kept her here for the whole session. I sat close to two foreign women. One was from India; her name was Ritu, a social activist who was dressed in full apparel, and her skeptical personality told how passionately she had been doing her job. The other woman was from Kansas, USA: Karen was a university administrator. At the other corner of the room, there was a slender Thai young man who covered his face with a beard and moustache that were a bit overdone and gave the impression that he was trying to make himself look a bit older than he actually was. He was a doctoral student studying education in the USA.

In general, "Different and Various" are words that could capture the impression one might have had of members of the group on that afternoon.

After three or four minutes of silence and a minute of me fumbling around with lighting switches in the back, a soothing voice could be heard telling everyone to open their eyes, to start reflecting on this earlier activity and to give feedback and share their feelings of being together in the same place and same time. We were not to forget the molecules of the air in the room that we kept breathing in and out, circulating from one's lung to another's.

'It is not peaceful, ' a young lad with a shining face spoke at length. He seemed hardly over thirty. 'First, I felt good, when the speaker told us to close our eyes. And I felt relaxed following his leading voice. However, after a while, I was getting annoyed by the noises of turning on and off the lights, wondering why it hadn't been stopped yet.'

A voice rose in agreement, one of his fellow college friends, but, this time, it was a woman in a plain dress. Her dress reflected her wish to live a life of humility in this world, to exist in harmony without harming innocent lives, which may seem insignificant and may be barely visible to eyes that are blind merely because they look upon those who are from a lower caste.

During our reflection, I observed that the contemplation resulted in the atmosphere in the room being as heavy as if a black velvet shroud was slowly pulled close, having covered all the stuff in the room. Master Prasart Pratesrut was sitting at the table corner, nodding his head and giving no indication of his own responses. His concern was focused on listening carefully. This determination to listen was so strong that it seemed to make the flying mosquitoes avoid intercepting his line of sight, with the considerate deference of saving him from being distracted by such low living things as they. Or, even if it was not so, the mosquitoes may have decided to fly elsewhere because they had a hidden agenda to taste blood from a leg or arm somewhere in the room.

When the heavy curtain of contemplation had covered us all, our reflection stretching long into the imaginative land made me feel as if I was brought into some Arabic territory with Baragu smoke stinking up the atmosphere. The choking fog curtain then changed to a lighted dawn when Aunty Maying from Petchaburi said with a strong accent ... 'What is the subject the facilitator wants us to speak about?' She was to speak from her feelings; instead she was asking the facilitator, how was she SUPPOSED to feel?

As we work together in this second session to form our Resolutions, it is important for us to understand this question. Being a member of a minority group made her feel reserved and play the role of inferiority, where the one sitting at the end of the table has the superior power. Hers was not, as such, a case of naivete, because she genuinely did know how to play the game—fully believing that the superior-inferior game had to be played—especially when she was aware that the only reason she, as someone from a minority group, could show up here was that money had been paid through someone's patronage. Otherwise, she might very well be spending time raising her grandsons in her village, instead of sitting here yesterday. Her manner of speech, in the beginning, got stuck on the language patterns that people learn from our bureaucratic system, and this seemed out of place, especially here in our 'World Peace Congress' gathering.

After the engagement in courtesies, her preliminary talk disappeared quickly, as if she wanted to test people's reaction, feinting and bluffing in the way a Thai boxer always does in the first round of a fight. The boxer does almost nothing, except some fancy footwork, dancing around the floor. From then on until the time was up and the bell rang, she revived and transformed as if a strange and foreign accent had pierced the air. She called for the God of Ghosts to decorate the settled area of the square room, where about half an hour earlier the organizer's team had refused to remove tables just to make it look less official.

'I am a Song Laotian but everyone calls me a "Stupid Laotian."' While she moved her body, her eyes glittered as if she were a wild tiger ready to play with her unfortunate victims. 'I studied a little. You guys here are full of knowledge and ability. When I looked at all of you, I thought of the small kids in my village. I was lucky to have more education than they had. I was the first one of the tribe who graduated with a Bachelor degree. Now, I am getting fairly old, but I still ask them to let me return to teach the children. I went back to the school to just sit idly on the chair until someone asked me why I was there. I asked them whether I could teach. They allowed me to teach those children. After that, I always go to teach at that school. I had a chance to meet some teachers and new children who were watching the screen all day long just like that person. When you want to talk, you still need to turn on a computer, instead of looking at my face. I also believe that I need to learn new things so I can talk to children with understanding.'

After the turning of heads and the stream of her voice ended, the doctorate student in education, who had flown back home from the

USA for his vacation, gradually and hesitatingly turned off his new Macbook and slowly inserted it into a nice leather bag as though it were a luxury ornament created by a popular designer. He kept his pose so that one could not tell his feelings; his face seemed unresponsive while he kept on listening silently.

Some of the audience with notebooks may not have heard her monologue; they were busy pressing buttons on their keyboards, hanging their heads low and staring at LCD screens as if any moment now on that screen an answer would pop up, and it would be the ultimate answer that would explain away all the secrets of life and our inhabited universe.

As we consider these observations of yesterday's session, let us ask ourselves a question:

Do the aesthetics of touch discriminate amongst human beings? Is delicacy of feeling a more powerful dividing line than races and ethnicity?

We must consider how our senses separate us and bring us together.

While the audience was talking in Thai, two female foreigners plugged in headsets to listen to the interpretation. The voice sounded like a babbling fish, translating every single word from Thai into English. All the consonants were interpreted into other consonants in the other language system. The interpreter was sitting at the back of the room conveying messages in English in a soft voice through a microphone. One of her ears seemed to lie low in order to focus on the listening while her mouth continued speaking non-stop. I was curious to know, between listening and speaking, which skill was the more important for her. How amazing it was that she was able to translate from one language into the other while listening to the first at the same time.

This was what I've always doubted. Human beings like us have tried hard to communicate with one another through different languages to achieve better understanding. I wonder, why exactly do people need to understand the meanings of other languages? Furthermore, with this attempt, why do we still have wars in the world? Why aren't we able to bring peace to our world yet? These are the questions I am asking as we write our Panel's Resolutions.

It would be better if the meanings we wish to convey could reach directly to the others' hearts without interpretation. Just imagine equating language interpretation to a medicine tablet or injected liquid. Whenever we need to communicate lengthily in any language, we could just swallow the tablets or inject the fluid into the body or veins. I say this on the assumption that it is possible that an understanding can be matched to the original meaning.

It is akin to perceiving the dew drops on the chin of the grass and acknowledging that it is beautiful and worthy for any man in the world to take time for a more focused observation, at least for a while. Another may pass by the same place and swear that the dew has soaked wet his very expensive shoes.

In the world of reality, however, there are no magic medicines. Yet, I have discovered something similar. 'Art' has the ability to do so. The effect of art is not art itself. When people communicate what they know, it will never be clear to the media. When they create works of art, the 'Fine Art' creators know well what they show is not the final answer, but a feeling. Probably, a piece of poetry composed by Maya Angelou, a dark skinned American poet and writer, will represent what I feel.

'A bird doesn't sing because it has an answer, it sings because it has a song.'

After everyone in the room had finished expressing all their feelings, Master Prasart spoke out slowly, resonantly and rhythmically as though he chanted a holy mantra. 'I would like us to notice that, at the first session, we started closing our eyes and listened to my speaking. That moment was the time upon which we concentrated as ourselves and with our own feelings. The temperature in the room was cool. Our minds were not disturbed by anything, but later on, when external factors such as when the lights inside were turned on and off, these began to be noticed, and we felt something unusual. The normality of our mind's state began to change. "Dissatisfaction" was induced into our minds, and it would become "dislike". Our minds disliked what was going on. Waves of thoughts co-arose with the question of why it had to be like that and not the other way around. This cycle repeated for many rounds until it reached one point when the peace in our minds disappeared altogether. Only irritated feelings now remained'.

At this moment, Master Prasart was giving me a quick look. I knew immediately what he wished me to do, since we have been working together for a long time. So I rose and walked to the flip chart board with a blank paper. I drew three small circles on the paper. The smallest circle was inside followed by the middle and then the largest circle. They all had the same center point at the middle of the concentric circles.

This can be represented roughly with a graphic similar to a dartboard:

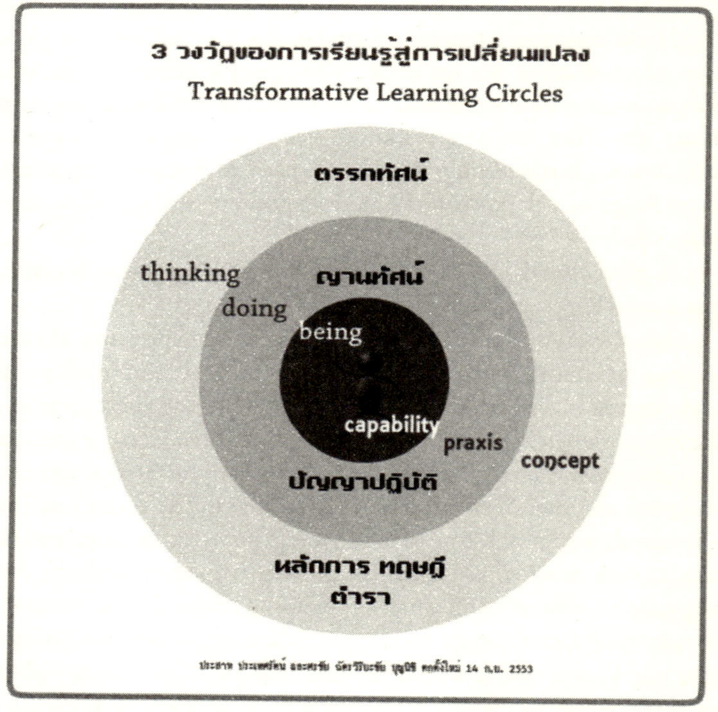

Then, as the session's moderator, Master Prasart, invited everyone to share their expectations for this World Peace Congress meeting, and we exchanged ideas widely. The dialogue accelerated to higher levels of participation, and this led to sufficient cooperation and the general perception that everyone's opinions were all intentionally heard. I have had lots of experiences in dialogue group settings and my sixth sense told me that the talk was not going to be an ordinary one.

Ms. Meena, an androgyne, told us about her direct experience of living in a barren area which was far beyond modern facilities. She found that in her life it was not too hard to find peace in her mind. On the other hand, being in the midst of modern equipment and facilities, we feel too far from peace. The chaos of routine daily life has dispersed the peace in our mind. This automatically popped up questions in my mind about what we humans actually need.

At this point, Aunty Maying narrated to us an anecdote of her childhood days. Simple happiness could be found from taking turns pushing friends down into the pond. There was only one simple rule they abided by: anyone who was pushed down into the water wouldn't get angry with anyone. If they got upset, nobody would play with them. We can say that co-habitation has been a skill or changing process, influenced by cultural roots. The real Thai root, in fact, refuses all violence. It is similar to the principles of the great man of India, Mahatma Gandhi: Satyagraha and Non-Violence (resulting in Civil Disobedience). It may not be fair if we blame the Western world for being the one to bring in capitalist ideals and influence us to value material things rather than the mind. It would be better if we looked back and blamed ourselves than to bow down and admit defeat by such alluring and pleasing powers. We should realize that the devil would not have been able to usurp our rights if we had not previously signed a contract with him in blood, even if we did so in ignorance.

Of course, it's no use leaving our hope with dead cultures. We can be influenced easily if we do not adjust ourselves to the times. However, a living culture was being presented to us yesterday by Mother Maying, a Lao Song lady, representing hundreds of lives in the villages and those who normally get up early in the morning at 4 or 5 a.m. to donate some steamed rice for the monks' alms. What do these elderly grandparents know, which we haven't yet discovered? Why have they continued this practice for ages? For those who have expressed their intention to conserve culture with superficial, overnight efforts, it could be said that they were only accomodating outsiders, who try to transform culture into merchandise and services in order to support the needs of wealthy people.

In the world of business, mass production is a typical way to make companies more convenient. If corporate executives didn't bow their heads and discuss matters closely, they would know as little as the typical customer. If we do not bow down to get along with them, we will become like people who build walls that extend artificial barriers between us and other human races, communities or neighbors who share the same fence or a mango tree's shade at the corner of the hedge. The idea of discrimination leads us to create violence in our minds. Separation is extremely hostile to peace. War that exists in the heart will burn more than an external war because we cannot escape it. It infests our very breathing ...

World peace begins from internal peace ...

This implication was repeatedly put forth during our first session, and it must be the core of our discussion today. 'His' voice and 'her' voice, both Thai and English, had spoken. The languages went back and forth discussing this topic. We talked about the rights of the media and information access. Whenever anyone in the room expressed themselves, and their ideas quite closely complied with our own concepts, I would write them down in the outside circle. If someone spoke out from their direct experiences or their practical wisdom, I would put these thoughts in the middle circle.

The knowledge we read in textbooks seemed far from reality. The faults of such knowledge became clear in the context of the presentation. It was a concept to which my colleagues and I ascribed little importance. When these ideas are once transformed into practice, with good discipline, it will then become clearer what we are doing with explicit knowledge; the process is just like acquiring the skill of riding a bicycle. Once we could ride a bicycle, we would never forget how to ride it because it became our capability. Such knowledge is practical, applicable and relevant to our lives. We would have transformed from those who could not do, to those who could. When we look at the circle chart, it may not be exaggerating facts to say that we value the practice of wisdom rather than knowledge from theory and texts.

When the process of thinking or theory is transferred to praxis, respecting and honoring one another will be then develop because the practices and community values have been accepted. Community members start, willingly, to learn, and the beauty of existence amidst diversity then appears ....

Many people have talked about embracing differences which may be actually valuable as a principle concept. They boast about it to show how smart they are. However, when they are facing their own experiences, they feel irritated and frustrated. This frustration could make the internal peace in their minds disappear even as they support the world peace initiative of our Congress.

At lunchtime, at the break during our first session, I was looking around to find anyone I could join at the table. A group of young university students who had volunteered to interpret were sitting together at the long table. They were chatting loudly according to their age and expressing their excitement in the new atmosphere. If we were looking for world peace, I would say that the atmosphere in this dining room, at that moment, was the best place to find it. Each person could choose his seat freely where he preferred.

Of course, many who were familiar with each another sat together. We possess instincts of avoiding differences and seeking something familiar to make us more comfortable. This is normal as human habits go. Once we sleep, we continue dreaming of such familiar things as we are normally used to in our waking behavior. So powerful is our routine habit in our daily lives that sometimes we have to train ourselves to act against what we feel is familiar. We should educate ourselves not to get stuck in the uncertainty and try to eliminate our laziness embedded in our inborn instincts to understand individual behavior. This mind mission needs to be solved first, before we were going to cross the line to achieve 'the World Peace'.

At that time, I saw Karen and Ritu looking for their seats; I then invited them to join my table. After we had been eating for a while, we start talking about typical questions such as how participants felt attending the conference and their opinions on my process which had been just finished. Karen said the same thing that Ritu wanted to say, coincidentally. She said ...

'How can you guys work together without speaking to each other? We didn't hear you say a word. How could you communicate? How did you know what the other needed? You seemed to understand each other as though you were the same person.'

Their faces showed both their appreciation and surprise.

'Of course, we talked but with no sound, ' I answered slowly in an alien language, touching my chest with one hand and said ... '...'cause we used the language of the heart.'

This is the language we must use as we write our Resolutions.

Panel VI: Modernism, Tradition and Eurocentrism

Tung-Yi Kho

This panel seeks to connect the issues of modernism, tradition and Eurocentrism to concerns of war and peace. In this brief essay, I will share what I understand by the term 'Eurocentrism.' Owing to space limitations, this account of Eurocentrism will necessarily be incomplete; it will attempt to highlight Eurocentrism's essential features and discuss how the topic is pertinent to our peace-related concerns. At the end, I offer some very general suggestions about what we may do to resist it in the interest of constructing a more peaceful human future.

I. What is Eurocentrism?

I would argue that Eurocentrism is foremost an orientation which regards Western civilization and culture, broadly defined, as superior to all other modes of being. Eurocentrism is so pervasive that it influences mainstream consciousness globally. And it is not merely ideational, abstract or intangible insofar as it pervades our structures of knowledge and consciousness, it is also material since such consciousness manifests in the institutions (social, cultural, economic, political) that govern our everyday existence.

Because it forms an all-encompassing milieu, Eurocentrism tends often to escape our attention. This is the challenge that it poses: its presence is obscured from our consciousness and so escapes identification. Nevertheless, it would seem apparent enough that quite irrespective of where we are in the world—be it Bangalore, Bangkok, or Beijing—we often find ourselves in a physical, institutional and symbolic milieu in which Euro-American conventions are taken for granted as the standard by which we deem the things of virtue, truth and beauty. One only has to reflect on the taken-for-grantedness of Western dress codes in the non-West to appreciate this fact. The same may be said about how 'natural' urban life, motorized transportation, market economies, the rule of law, et cetera, have come to be. Such is the pervasiveness of Eurocentrism.

Moreover, these examples should adequately highlight that Eurocentrism is not a phenomenon confined to politics, economy, education, the law and the arts taken separately. Rather, Eurocentrism is a certain consciousness that infuses all these realms *in toto*, simultaneously. It is a corpus of knowledge and beliefs that informs, shapes and gives life to our ideas of sociation, of how we should live with and relate to one another. Again, this reminds us that Eurocentrism does not exist merely in the realm of ideas: it is material insofar as these ideas manifest in the material, institutional structures of our everyday world.

Another way perhaps to understand and illustrate Eurocentrism would be to evaluate common responses to the following: What is beauty, truth, goodness, progress, development, freedom, et cetera? It would be apparent that the sentiments ordinarily evoked by such a query would smack of Euro-American influence. Indeed, Eurocentrism at its most fundamental is the syndrome in which Euro-American historical experience is considered to be the template of development for all peoples around the globe. In this schema, Euro-America is thought of as the crucible of human development, licensed to have the last word on what the latter should constitute. This belief—preponderant in the non-West as much as in the West—explains Eurocentrism's all-encompassing nature and its inflection in all spheres of human activity.

II. The Implications of Eurocentrism

There is no space here for an account of how Eurocentrism became the ubiquitous phenomenon it is (although any satisfactory attempt would undoubtedly have to take issue with the inroads made by colonialism and the modern mass media). As such, I hope only to consider the implications of a world under the sway of a Eurocentric order, which appears already to be the world situation. In what has been euphemistically called 'globalization', immense efforts have been and are being invested to incorporate increasing sections of the world's population into the modern-capitalist world economy. The purported goal—though not readily acknowledged—is to re-make the world in the image of the West. The desirability of this project is often implicitly assumed and unquestioned: it constitutes 'development'. In fact, the promise of Western lifestyles and standards of living means that the project of 'globalization' is sometimes pursued more vigorously by non-Western people than by its proponents in the West.

Nevertheless, even if it were so desired, can the entire world replicate the historical experience and achieve the living standards of Euro-America? Gandhi responded to such a prospect by highlighting the violent, exploitative and zero-sum nature of industrialization and Western civilization. He forewarned, 'God forbid that India should ever take to industrialism after the manner of the West. The economic imperialism of a single tiny island kingdom (England) is today keeping the world in chains. If an entire nation of 300 million took to similar economic exploitation, it would strip the earth bare like locusts.' (20-12-1928). Elsewhere, Gandhi noted, 'To make India like England and America is to find some other races and places of the earth for exploitation. So far it appears that the Western nations have divided all the known races outside Europe for exploitation and that there are no new worlds to discover.' (7-10-1926).

III. Eurocentrism, War, and Peace

Gandhi's observations above are instructive and significant, for they leave no doubt as to (i) the origins of the wealth of England (and Europe, more generally) and (ii) the costs of Western industrialisation, two issues over which considerable mystification exists. To be sure, Gandhi understood that the accomplishment of so-called Western civilization (modernity, industrialization et cetera) was made possible only through imperialism and the pillage and exploitation of Europe's colonies: 'inferior' races, women and nature. The relationship between

Western civilization and war was therefore laid bare. Its pursuit was inherently exploitative and violent. Carried to its practical ends, Eurocentrism—as the belief in the superiority of Western civilization—implies incessant war.

It is important to note that this insight stands in stark contrast to mainstream beliefs, which are typically Eurocentric in that they explain Europe's rise to factors internal to it while downplaying or omitting altogether the role of European colonialism. This ignores the violence associated with industrial modernization and tends instead to cast it as a far more benign process.

Two important consequences have emerged from this obfuscation: first, is the myth that modernization can be pursued by all at no or little cost; second, modernity (and its accoutrements) became the universal end-point of human development. By the turn of the mid-twentieth century, industrialization/modernization had become the unequivocal goal of all nation-states and nationalist projects. The viability of the continued expansion of the industrial mode of life was seldom called into question and Gandhi's admonishment was mostly ignored. However, physical realities cannot simply be wished away.

Today, the contemporary world is one that is furnished with the accoutrements of Modernity: it is decidedly industrial and capitalist and, thanks to 'globalization', it is a mode of existence that has expanded into the far reaches of the globe. Europe has rather successfully carved up the world in its own image. It has become a univalent Eurocentric world-order for the most part, economically, politically and culturally, and so we speak of the pandemic of Eurocentrism. And, perhaps as such, it is a world that is perched precariously on a knife's edge, where peace seems, now more than ever, to be a chimera, and where war is the rule rather than the exception. Today, as the countries of the developed world find themselves lurching from one economic crisis to another, the developing countries, which are entrenched in the periphery of the system, are forced as a matter of survival to make (structural) adjustments to render themselves attractive to the custodians of capital in a life-and-death competition with one another. And this is to say nothing about the ecological crisis that threatens all planetary life.

There is neither security nor stability in a Eurocentric milieu.

IV. Resisting Eurocentrism

Eurocentrism and the mode of existence it seeks to impose (modernity) are therefore antithetical to peace. It is an orientation predicated on exploitation, expropriation and violence. Furthermore, the violence that Eurocentrism entails is not merely nebulous in the form of cultural domination but can and has been overt, tangible and immediate. In fact, such overt violence in the form of military and colonial domination has tended to be the precursor to less 'tangible' forms of coercion historically; in other words, 'hard' military-political dominance makes possible the more 'subtle' forms of coercion and cultural dominance among them.

But what can we do? How can we resist Eurocentrism to forge a more meaningful and peaceful human existence? And how can we do this given that almost all of us have in some way or other been inundated and infected by it since birth? Our panel will issue more formal propositions in a separate document. For a start, however, I will propose that we recognize Eurocentrism for what it is and bring to self-consciousness our (often unwitting) complicity in its perpetuation. In addition, we should strive to re-discover and revive the multitudinous ways of existence known to human beings since the beginning of time. There is therefore the need to examine the traditions of our forebears. It goes without saying that cultural diversity should be actively promoted and appreciated. After all, we should remember that there is more than one way to be human.

Panel VII: Science, Cosmology and Metaphysics

Prasad Meetam

1. Introduction

I was invited to give a lecture at the third 'World Peace Congress'[1]. The purpose of the third congress, as stated in its website, was ' to create a face-to-face dialogue that is contemporary and sustainable amongst groups of individuals who are different in their thought processes, vision, interests and ideology that have divided society into differing sections'.[2]

The goal of this meeting focuses on building the basis for a dialogue that is continuing and sustainable, so that there will be **an exchange of learned lessons for all humanity.** Khun Surasri Kosolnavin, the president of the Sathien Koses–Nagaprateep Foundation, who is the organizer and the president of the meeting, designated 12 topics for discussion.

When I was asked to participate as co-lecturer on the topics of Science, Cosmology, and Metaphysics, I turned down the invitation immediately because I am a mathematician with some knowledge of science but not enough to make the talk interesting, and I don't know anything at all about the other two subjects.

I added, **'But I have followed the subject of energy for the past ten years, and I would like to state firmly and directly that if there is no new energy policy, on both the global and national levels, there can be no peace anywhere on earth.'**

And with no hesitation, I took the opportunity to explain the subject to the coordinator.

After about 4–5 hours, the same coordinator called me again and said, **'I have related your reasons to the team in the US; they said this is what they want and that they would also like to hear specifically about difficult cases in Thailand.'**

After the coordinator and her team agreed with me, I was worried because I am not proficient enough in the English language, but she told me, 'Not to worry, we have an interpreter to help you out.'

My apologies for being long-winded but this is evidence to show that it is only now people are beginning to agree with me on what I have tried to call attention to for many years. That is to say, world peace and that of Thailand will never be realized as long as there is no new energy policy.

What happened has encouraged and given me confidence that all the 'fan clubs' feel the same way as I do. We can stand firm only when we are determined and strong, not distracted by outside influences.

I have also searched the website (http://worldpeacecongress.info/thai/program.html) and found, in the World Peace Congress documents, a quote from Mahatma Gandhi, that says, **'You must be the change you want to see in the world.'**

2. What is peace? What are the indicators for peace?

I would like to begin by telling a story of how a math instructor, who should concern himself only with all those difficult-to-understand symbols, has turned his attention to energy policy. Almost ten years ago, an elderly lady from Jana District (not Mrs. Nium) spoke up at a meeting of villagers who were protesting the gas pipeline project and the Thailand-Malaysia gas extraction plant. She said, **'We are villagers, we have no knowledge. You are learned, don't be lazy. You help get us the information, and we'll consider it ourselves.'** I still remember what I was thinking then when I heard the words, **'Don't be lazy, ... and we'll consider it ourselves.'** Since then, I have acquired knowledge from individuals and from the Internet, and collected many articles, enough to fill 5–6 books, not counting many hundreds of unpublished articles.

In a small group talk at that time, there were about 20 listeners.

During the introduction, one person said that, 'I'm a businesswoman from abroad. I've thought of coming back to live in Thailand so many times, but have then gone back to the foreign country every time. I'm also considering it again this time but am still hesitant. The reason I'm attending this meeting is because a friend who is sitting next to me asked me to come.'

On the third day, which was the last day, she and her friend told me that, 'We are very impressed with your lecture.' I thanked her and asked, 'When are you going back abroad?'

'I've decided not to go but will go to work in Phuket helping those who have problems there. May I have your e-mail address so we can correspond?' I didn't know **'what she thought (for herself).'** But this is a result of Gandhi's words, **'You must be the change you want to see in the world.'**

My apologies once again for the digression but, I believe, it is still within the realm of the 'World Peace' conference. I would like to go directly to the point by presenting brief quotes from two very important world figures.

The first person is the Dalai Lama who said, **'Peace means happiness.'** However, what is 'Happiness'? It cannot be just an abstract saying; there must be a reasonably clear indicator. I utilized the approach that either Socrates or Plato (I can't quite remember) had used in teaching philosophy thousands of years ago.

Where should we then begin the movement for creating world peace?

Mother Theresa, who was also a Nobel Peace Prize recipient, as was the Dalai Lama, has said, **'Peace begins from a single smile.'** I agreed and was very impressed with the saying, but it is not 'adequate' for the very complex and varied contemporary world.

I would like to point out the standard of measurement from Bhutan[3] which has created the Gross National Happiness Index (GNH). According to Bhutan's GNH, there are 9 components in complete happiness, which are as follows.

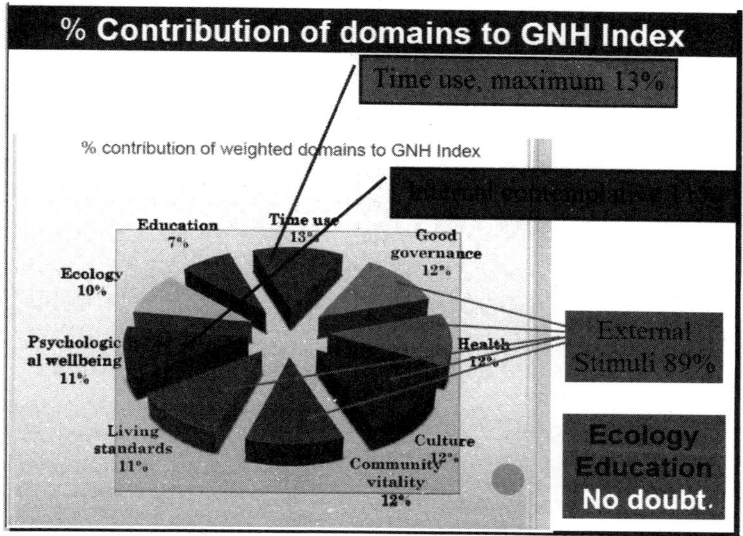

Time Use by people has the most importance and consequently a weight of 13%. It details how humans utilize their time: for example, how many hours for sleeping. If it is too few, then there is less happiness. Leisure time or time to appreciate nature is also considered. The factor which has the least importance, at only 7%, is education.

The other seven factors are, good governance (at 12% and addressing such issues as corruption, democratization, good services from government officials), health (at 12% and encompassing, for example, longevity), culture (at 12% and referring to family relationships, etc.), community vitality (at 12% and including participation or helping others, etc.), standard of living (11%), psychological well-being (11%), and ecology (10%).

In all, internal factors that contribute to the GNH index are only 11% and the rest, 89%, comes from the outside, from environmental stimuli.

When peace is happiness (according to the Dalai Lama) and 89% of 100% of happiness comes from outside, therefore peace is all about external stimuli. I will respectfully submit in the following that these stimuli come mainly from the energy policy of the government.

3. What is world crisis (or what is opposite to world peace) and what is the cause of it?

3.1 World Crisis

To see the dynamic changes in the world, I compare analyses of two different individuals who are separated by 44 years.

The first individual is Dr Martin Luther King (who received the Nobel Peace Prize in 1964). He stated that there are three categories of world crises: **(1) injustice between races, (2) poverty and (3) war.**

Forty-four years afterwards, Susan George, who was world-renowned for being anti-capitalism, added two more categories which are **financial crises and global warming (including destruction of plants and animals).**

In fact, what Susan George had in mind for the two categories was what amounted to war without having to use guns or explosives, but using capitalism and **energy policy** as invisible weapons instead. I didn't easily come to this conclusion on my own, but there are reasons for my deductions which I will explain later.

3.2 What is the cause?

I presented the small group meeting with cartoons and newspaper clippings (but I won't present them here) to show that, after the US armed forces successfully seized President Saddam's palace (2003), people looted valuables from the palace, while President George Bush unashamedly took over the oil rigs in Iraq.

Three years later (2007), Alan Greenspan, former Chairman of the U.S. Federal Reserve, disclosed that the war in Iraq was waged because the U.S. wanted oil.

We can conclude at this point that the Iraq war was about the need for energy sources among the people who had the authority to decide to go to war. Those persons could include the US President (an oil industrialist), or the Secretary of State, (Dr. Condoleeza Rice, former president of Chevron, the oil merchant that is going to drill for oil in the area around Samui Island, one of our main tourist destinations).

As for the causes of the greenhouse effect and the destruction of plants and animals, I have presented evidence and scientific data which show that, among the greenhouse gases that humans have manufactured (which is the cause of the greenhouse effect), 72% is from carbon dioxide, the other 28% is composed of 18% methane (which comes from plant decay) and about 9% nitrous oxide (which comes from chemical fertilizers used in agriculture).[4]

We have found that 91% of carbon dioxide comes from fossil fuel used in production by humans. The principal producers are power plants (30%), industry (21%), transportation (19%), housing and commercial building (13%) and fossil-based energy production (8%).

To state it succinctly, 66% of greenhouse gases that humans produce comes from fossil fuel (that is coal, oil and natural gas).

Let us review at this point that energy leads to (1) war and (2) global warming that is wreaking havoc all over the world, including destruction to plants, animals and infrastructure, with increasing violence such as no one could have anticipated.

Nicholas Stern, former Vice President of the World Bank, made it crystal clear that '[c]**limate change (or global warming) is the most serious marketing mistake that the world population has ever experienced.**' He further explained and offered a solution: '**Our generation's dependency on fossil fuel today is a danger that the next generation has not been informed of. Alternative sources of energy are the best answer to the security of air, energy, and the economy.**'

Here we have the third component, which is **the security of the economy**. Readers please go back to see what the components of the Happiness Index (which means the Peace Measurement Index) are. Besides the three categories of world crisis, that is, (1) war, (2) global warming and (3) economic security, there are many other factors relating to world peace. We will examine them in the case of Thailand.

4. Crisis in Thailand

In addition to the crisis in the world as discussed above, permit me to add other problems that make peace impossible. We will now discuss the problems in Thailand.

Today's energy problem creates conflict at a local level. I can cite three cases that have been in the news for a long time: Pakmoon Dam, Bornok-Bangrud coal power plant in Prachuabkirikhan province and the Thai-Malay gas pipeline and gas extraction plant in Jana district, Songkhla province.

I'll begin with a picture of police looking at the villagers at Pakmoon Dam, Ubonrachathani province. The government built the dam to produce hydro-power. As a result, more than 1, 700 families were relocated, 6, 200 households lost their source of income since the fishery route was blocked and 116 species (44%) have disappeared. The fishery now produces only 20% of what it used to. Let me tell you that I once met a villager from Pakmoon selling grilled eggs along the Smila beach in Songkhla province because of the problem at Pakmoon Dam.

The next picture is a confrontation between the Assembly of the Poor and the police, followed by pictures of a mother with an infant being arrested and put in the police wagon and an elderly man with blood streaming from cuts on his head. Another photo shows people lighting incense for Khun Charoen Wad-aksorn, the protest leader who was assassinated, because of his involvement in a protest against the construction of a coal power plant in Prachuabkirikhan province. I would like to submit to the assembly here that I was standing nearby when this particular photo was taken. Khun Charoen, whom I'd call a 'true citizen', had pointedly explained to us the government's view on the subject that, **'there is only coal in these people's brains.'**

The last two pictures show incidents surrounding the Thailand-Malaysia gas pipeline in Songkhla province. There is a woman with blood on her face being helped by the police during the public comment event (only people who supported the pipeline were allowed to attend). The photo that shows four women standing in a cage came from an incident where the police tried to block the attempt of people who wanted to present a letter of protest during the government of Thaksin Shinnawat (20 December 2002)

At present, the District Court and the Appeals Court have already ruled that the people were not guilty. It has been almost ten years and the Royal Thai Police has appealed to the Dika Court. The case is still pending there.

I can briefly describe the steps of the conflict: it began with the government's project focusing on finding energy. The people were afraid of the impact from the project, they protested it and fought with the police. There were people who were injured, imprisoned or killed. What can we do to help Thai society to be free of this cycle?

I have given information on the hydro-electricity dam and electricity usage to those who never knew that: '**the amount of electricity that the three big shopping malls, Ma Boonkrong, Siam Paragon, and Centralville, use is equal to the amount of electricity produced by three dams, Pakmoon, Sirindhorn, and Ubolrat, or the amount that people in Mae Hong Sorn and Ranong provinces use altogether.**'

In other words, we moved people out of an area to build a dam which affected these people to the point that they were almost bankrupt, so that customers in department stores can feel cool and comfortable, and they can use escalators instead of stairs. I would like to ask the audience: '**do you think that peace can happen in such an unjust society?**'

On the topic of inequality in Thailand, I would like to move from the local level to an overall picture of the country, and to energy and the overall economy. In 1993, Thailand spent 11.3% of GDP on energy but in 2008, the expenditure increased to 18.7%. Although the expenditure on energy is almost 20% of the GDP, employment in the energy sector was less than one percent of the 34 million strong work force. This figure includes almost two hundred thousand gas station workers (who are very poor). Moreover, expenditures on renewable energy (which is difficult to monopolize, such as firewood, charcoal) has decreased from 2.1% to 1.4% of GDP during the same period.

On the subject of environment, a survey of dissolved oxygen (DO) in fresh water areas of 114 countries indicates that Thailand has the lowest DO which is 2.98 milligram/liter. This is a level at which it is difficult for fish to survive (fish need DO at a value of 5 mg/liter to grow and reproduce).

Therefore, not only can energy be a cause for war, global warming, conflict in communities, conflict between the state and the people and destruction of the resource base, sources of food and livelihood for the people, it is also a source of employment problems or unemployment.

As for the gap between the rich and the poor which Susan George said is a global crisis, the latest survey result of a United Nations agency[5] found that while the income gap between the rich and the poor in Japan and Scandinavian countries is about three or four times (the rest of Europe is 5–8 times, and 9–11 times in Southeast Asian countries), it is 13–15 times in Thailand.

Walden Bello, [6] a famous intellectual (the author of the book, *A Siamese Tragedy: Development and Disintegration in Modern Thailand*), wrote that, **'Poverty is a phenomenon almost everywhere in the rural areas in Thailand.'** This is one of the causes of conflict between groups of colored shirts in Thailand. It is regrettable that the public lacks clarity when reflecting on the problem.

What I have related so far is the past that is still with us today. Some of you might optimistically think that it was a past mistake and we should move on. Society and bureaucracy have learned their lessons and history will not repeat itself. In fact, that has not happened. Right now there are plans to build 9 coal power plants and 5 nuclear power plants.

One of these will be in the sub-district of my hometown.

I had stated that, 'Before coming to Nakhonnoyak, I had talked with people who protested the construction of coal power plant ... they wanted to build a plant that has 700 megawatt capacity even though people in the three provinces, Nakorn Srithammarat, Trang, and Pattalung, combined, use less than 300 megawatts.' And to see the 'new energy policy' in concrete terms of how it will help return peace to communities and the world, I would like to submit that: *'The people of Hua Sai district (where the coal power plant is situated) use only 7 megawatts. If we do not import coal from abroad, we can use firewood instead. The people can plant trees for firewood and sell them locally, saving transportation costs. The revenue that can be realized is estimated to be about 100 million Baht a year. There will be jobs and no need to migrate to the cities to sell grilled eggs or drive motorcycle taxis ... Isn't this the route to peace which means happiness and security?'*

Besides small group discussions, I also had an opportunity to present to the whole assembly (in place of the chairs of other groups who were unable to participate due to urgent business). Those who were at the meeting asked questions on nuclear power plants. My answer was 'nuclear power plants can't mitigate the problem of global warming, because not only it will take 12 years, we would also need additional energy from fossils. The problem of global warming must be dealt with now.' To be succinct, I quoted former Vice President Al Gore who said that, *'If we were able to solve two important problems (supposedly), which is (1) how to store nuclear waste safely and (2) how to prevent the terrorists from getting nuclear weapons (which can be built very easily) would we still be wondering if the nuclear power plant is worth the investment?'*

I would add that the Thai government has spent 1, 200 million Baht on a public relations campaign promoting the positive aspects of nuclear power plants, including invitations to the media and academicians to go on a fact-finding trip abroad. But there was no money at all for groups that oppose the project. Is this fair to Thai people who want to know the truth?

5. What is the new energy policy?

There are three main factors to consider: economy, security (and sustainability) and compatibility with communities and environment. These three factors are called the 'triangle of energy policy'.

I want to expand the broad outline above with a poster from Africa that says, 'Renewable Energy Is Peoples' Power.'

The posters that people in the photos were holding (we couldn't read them—but I have enlarged them), ask, 'we have the sun, but why don't we have jobs', 'sustainable energy creates more jobs for us' and 'renewable energy is better for development from the bottom to the top because communities can participate'. Readers please compare this to the coal power plant example: how different it is, as different as the sky and the valley. Electricity from wind turbines doesn't use water, doesn't release waste water nor carbon dioxide and other poisonous gases. To state it more clearly, the new energy policy is called 'Feed-In Tariffs' or 'Feed-In Law'. The principle of the policy

is, from those who produce electricity from renewable energy (such as wind turbines solar panels (which can be on the roof of a small house), biomass (firewood, waste water, biogas), the state (or entrepreneur who operates the electricity cable) will automatically buy the electricity for a period of 20 years, at a price that is 'compassionate'.

For example, in the first five years, the buying price is higher than that of the last 15 years. Prices are lower for areas with strong wind than they are for those that are less windy. In areas such as the sea, if investment cost is higher, then the buying price is higher in order to keep the energy supply going without destroying the environment, or releasing carbon dioxide gas. With this policy, the use of solar panels in Germany had increased more than three-fold within 3 years of the law being passed. Overall, the production of electricity from renewable energy in Germany has increased from 11.8% (of the country's total production) in 2006 to 12.5% in 2010.

Thais spend 4.3 hundred thousand billion Baht a year on

electricity. Just imagine if only 10% of this could be produced from renewable energy, how much poverty in the rural areas would be reduced.

6. Changing the Policy to Reality: Beginning from the Bottom to the Top

I would like to pose a question: who should lead the change to solve the world crisis especially on global warming and war?

The shameful failure of the conference on global warming in Copenhagen, Denmark, which was supported by the United Nations, has shown us that people cannot pin their hopes on this international organization.

Why?

The first global warming conference was held in Norway in 1990 and the theme was 'Our Common Future'. From then on, until 2009, the amount of carbon dioxide in the atmosphere has increased by 40%, but negotiations have failed miserably. Moreover, many people from various countries who were affected directly (including Thailand) were arrested by the police.

This is because 51% of total carbon dioxide gas that was released came from the five permanent members of the UN Security Council (UNSC): which are China, the United States, Russia, England and France). It takes only one dissenting vote from these countries to block the resolution.

Why do we have the meeting then? So we can expose the problem to the world. I am answering my own question.

It is the same on the war front. That is to say, 95% of weapons and equipment for waging war in the world were also produced by the same five members of the UNSC.

7. Conclusion

From the aforementioned reasons, including other lessons learned from all over the world, we cannot hope to rely on the United Nations, nor on any government of a country. This is because the government of each individual country is no different from an energy broker or a merchant.

The approach of a civil society, both globally (with organizations such as World Peace Congress) and nationally, is to educate people. Someone has suggested that the theme, **'Think Globally, Act Locally'** should be adapted to, **'Talking Globally, Putting the Brakes on Nationally.'**

Yes! We must stop the nine coal power plants and five nuclear power plants.

This action is essential to the survival of humanity and all species of the world. Civil society groups around the world should connect ('Only Connect' according to the slogan of the World Peace Congress) to build peace for the world by putting the brakes on 'development' that only increases world crises.

Notes

1. The previous two Congresses were held in Salt Lake City, Utah, United States of America (August 2007), and in Bangalore, India (27 February–1 March 2009)
2. http://worldpeacecongress.info/history.html
3. From The Centre for Bhutan Studies (http://www.bhutanstudies.org.bt/)
4. http://en.wikipedia.org/wiki/File:Greenhouse_Gas_by_Sector.png
5. From an article titled, 'Inequality Gap Stains Thailand's MDG Achievements.' by Marwaan Mcan - Markar (May 10, 2010)
6. In an article titled, 'The Battle for Thailand'

Panel VII: Science, Cosmology, & Metaphysics

Kampanad Baktikul

Today's world needs science that is not merely the science of possession, exploitation of resources on earth and the universe with technological developments. Energy policies create war to fight for benefits. They stimulate global warming. The gap of inequality and conflict in the community is increased. Previously science was meant to study what is around us, but it ignored the essence of human beings. Contemporary scientific studies have to focus on mental and spiritual states of being that seek peace. It is important to sustain the world and its creatures. Cosmologically, we have already searched for resources from other planets. However, in the matter of oneself, the world still needs to search to see the genuine inner essence. Differences in concepts, belief in metaphysics and religion may cause conflicts within individuals and between individuals.

Introduction

Science is for mankind or for peace. Knowledge of things in nature, both living and nonliving, include empirical comprehensive processes called the scientific process (Pearl 2009); all types of knowledge from these processes are what we call 'science'. In general, the word 'Science' means 'exact science' which does not include Social Sciences, which have to use scientific process as well. Differences between the social sciences and 'exact' sciences are in terms of content and nature of the study, nothing else.

The word 'science' in English then has this dual meaning. We will use a definition in this article which includes natural science, applied science, health sciences and many branches of social science. Military science is also placed in this category. The direction of development in science and technology tends to be more coherent within military science than with the other sciences. It will branch more to create new in-depth knowledge for peace. All of science must be used to serve humanity, not just to meet the needs of people like in the past, regardless of the human essence.

While the global society and economy today are highly competitive at national, regional and global levels, there are other issues such as world economic integration, free trade, exploitation and seeking benefits from trade barriers, patented and patent infringement, environment and energy crisis, politics and governing of countries. Countries around the world will protect their own national interests. What can we do to create a self-sufficient society, a society without deprivation of human rights and a society that respects human dignity? We must stop the infringement of personal rights, respect right to life of individuals; since every person should have equality of life, at least it is the right of people to survive. People shall have the right to do what they should do and not to do anything to hurt themselves or others physically or mentally.

It is becoming increasingly important in the next decade to find out if there is any or where there is peace and peaceful geography on earth. Where is the world of peace and new world order? How can we start walking to reach that point? These are questions whose answers we must help each other to find.

In scientific cosmology, 'universe' refers to region, gathering, group and the vicinity of any world (The Royal Institute Dictionary 2542). Science is translated as knowledge, so cosmology means the knowledge of the world and what we find around the world. In English, cosmology is defined as 'the science of the origin and structure of the universe, especially as studied in Astronomy'.

'Cosmology' has two branches. The first branch is called scientific cosmology. It is the study of the universe as a whole. This study is considered as the greatest and most fundamental thing at the same time (Harrison 2000, Ryden 2003). This approach aims to study the composition of and the relationships among everything in the universe. It tries to explain how the universe in the past was and in the future will be and whether the universe is limited or not: How did the universe occur? Why does it take the shape it has today. People always have questions in their minds about where we come from, who we are and where we are going (Guaguin 1897). These questions are what interest all cosmologists, who believe they may be important keys to answers at the macro level. This requires knowledge from many fields such as astrophysics science, philosophy, religion and even art.

Despite what people know about the universe, it is still considered a very small amount of knowledge. Many questions in cosmology are still a mystery today. Even though the universe is vast, it is still the subject of the fire of human passion, and the object of our abuse. Misusing natural resources has resulted in greenhouse gas emissions. 'Global warming' and 'climate variability' have become catch phrases. They encapsulate the world. They are simple action rules. Man must accept the result of karma, according to karma and the circle of births and deaths described in Buddhist cosmology science.

Buddhist Cosmology

Most people believe that there is no real thing that they cannot see or touch. Most people also believe that once you die you're finished. You will not be reborn. They neither believe in the current world nor in the next world. The explanation of the current world and the next world appears in the *Tripitaka* which elucidatesthe correct meaning. It is the first of the Eight Noble Paths, divided into ten topics, which are the sum and substance of understanding life and the world. The current world and the next are together one of those topics. Both words are often used conjunction because they are related to each other. These beliefs strongly affect the cosmology of Buddhist Studies (Dhammakaya Open University 2008).

Scientific cosmology and Buddhist cosmology have different objectives and methods of study. Knowledge about the current world and the universe came from study and experiment with equipment and the scientific method. The study of nature is an incomplete knowledge. It changes all the time. The Buddha discovered the universe from natural law by the 'mind method'. This type of knowledge is called science. This knowledge does not change. Truly, science plays an important role in developing technology. We may say that science can bring material prosperity to human beings. Progress in science engenders the discoveries of natural laws of the world and the universe. It is just one way to make human knowledge clearer.

Buddhist cosmology clarifies knowledge in other ways. It is a discovery of the natural laws of the world and the universe under a different paradigm. It includes a way of study of the world, the universe and living things from the occurring, existing and decaying. Buddhist cosmology is a study of the reality of the universe from the teachings in the Theravada Buddhist scriptures. It is a warning to the student to attempt a proper understanding of the world and life. The meaning of the Buddhist world includes earth as creature, as a body and mind, and as a place to stay. Beyond those three understandings of the world, PhaThep Mongkol Muni (Sod Juntasaro) extends a further explanation: earth, understood as a creature, is a mind that is seeing, remembering, thinking about, and knowing all creatures. An additional explanation is that those three understandings of the world are groups of creatures such as living things. They are man, animal and human or non-human. All of these are creatures because they fall under the condition of occurring, existing and decaying or perishing eventually. Earth Khan is Khan 5 or the principle nature under the nature condition. It is bestowed with a figure, emotion, recognition, body and sprit of all creatures, human, god, Arupa Brahma until Gotrabhu Dhamma Body, Sotapanna Dhamma Body, Sakadagami Dhamma Body and Arahat Dhamma Body. World Climate is an environment starting from the environment around us and extending to stars in other universes. It keeps extending to the infinite universe without boundary. It is a habitat for the animals in that place. With the meanings that have been collected, we realise that the world is not meant only for living human beings and life but it also has profound meaning and other significances as well.

No matter how advanced the scientific becomes, it should be noted that today animals are still dying in large numbers. There are poultry, livestock and aquatic animals, et cetera that die from worldwide epidemics. A huge number of animals are killed to prevent the spread of the diseases such as SAR, avian flu and swine flu. People are killed by natural disasters, catastrophic floods, mudslides, tsunamis, earthquakes, volcanoes and new diseases that can be traced to climate change.

Is this because of karma, resulting from the Law of Karma? The law of nature is logical to the explanation of the Buddhist religion. It is said that fire within the hearts of men threatens to burn the outside world. The three fires are *Rakidkina* (fire of lust), *Toesukina* (fire of hatred) and *Mohuckina* (fire of delusion).

Rakidkina

Lust is fire. Lust is an ambitious longing in taste, odor, voice and touch. When it cannot be appreciated, it will cause a struggle to seek. Once we have got it, we will need it for more. It's never enough. A desire that may have been happy, ambitious and emotional in the past turns into a burning mind that yearns endlessly. Fire is lust. In accord with this meaning, monks who sought release practiced Buddhism. The lust that teaches people is called greed. It is an endless need and nothing is ever enough. Violation of the rights of others such as intrusion into public land, burning forests to occupy land, deforestation, destroying streams, the invasion into the mangrove, emissions from industry, regardless of morality and ethics have caused an encroachment into nature.

Toesukina

Hatred is fire. It is dissatisfaction or indignation, when people feel discontent or come and take anything that was desired by someone else first. It provokes ire and burns the mind at all times. If there is no patience there will have to be a fight. A little or a big war or battle, is not only caused by the greed but also anger. The situation of any one country and the world as a whole is embroiled in gunshots and explosions. Hatred keeps expanding and shows no sign of ending easily even whilst there is a question of 'Seeking for Peace' from other groups.

Mohuckina

Delusion is fire. It is an unknown factor in all conditions. It causes wrong thinking, wrong doing, wrong speaking and self-centeredness. It makes people feel that they are better than others. It makes people gloat over others worse off than themselves. It bares the ego. It is sometimes inanimate and sometimes distracted and cannot be controlled. It becomes a supporting factor for lust fire and rage fire to then become more intense. Delusion is the reason why people do evil things and then keep repeating their mistakes. It is delusion fire that blocks one from seeing things in their right sense. The world is then no less suffering because of these people ruled by delusion fire. As long as passions such greed, delusion and anger are still blazing in the human mind, the world will certainly be demolished (Dhamma Leela 2550).

Knowing this, science or technology that aims to study and seek resources to meet the needs of the people regardless of the human essence, could only be a science of destruction. From now on, contemporary science has to focus on studying the mind and spirit to find peace of mind and peace for the world.

Metaphysics

The word 'meta' means the greatest, the highest and the uppermost. Philosophy means decent knowledge. (*Pimpan Thep Su Metha Non*) When they are combined, metaphysics then means the philosophy related to the thing that is beyond the general sight or knowledge of any witness, but it could be known and understood by the reasons. Metaphysics is the science and essence of reality. Metaphysics is considered the first branch of pure philosophy occurring in the world. It occurs as a surprise and a question of ancient humans regarding natural phenomena and the environment. The curiosity of human beings incites them to find out the cause of those facts. Correct reality and fact are the basis of metaphysics.

The three main branches of metaphysics are materialism, idealism and naturalism. In addition to those three major branches of metaphysics, there is ontology which is an important branch of metaphysics. It is the science of being. These two are related because metaphysics is a science that talks about truth or substance as they exist. Ontology is a study of how the existence of truth or substance actually manifests. In general, these two sciences are considered as the same study. They contemplate upon the existence of the real or the real of existance. Ontology was split into three popular theories. They are monism, dualism and pluralism. Metaphysics is regarded as the main structure of philosophy. Devoid of metaphysics, philosophy could not exist. Using philosophy, it is necessary to mainly stick to the metaphysical structure.

1. Metaphysics, the materialist branch: This refers to the belief that substance or energy determines the basic characteristics of all things and events, but the substance is only a condition for existence. Apart from that, it is believed that there is no existence. 'Mental' or 'spiritual experience' does not exist. It is only a derivative condition which is caused by a substance or known as the output of the substance. Then materialism enters. Materialism has different meanings. It refers to the perspective of the science of ethics which is the belief that property, money and power is important because it can direct the most happiness to life. This is materialism ... and someone who is materialistic will perceive life this way.

Materialistic people consider everything to be of substance or material. Materialism was recognized by early Greek philosophy, which tried to find answers regarding the world and everything that appears in it. One such answer was that the world is created out of earth, water, air and fire. When these four elements are combined, then everything happens. This approach assumes that the object or substance arises from the bonding of countless atoms. Objects or a substance, when divided into segments until they cannot be divided anymore, are called atoms. Atomism believes the truth that only a substance exists. This material can be divided into the smallest scale called the atom (or atomic). The word atom in philosophy refers to the smallest particles. It is the final particle that can no longer be separated. The atom is eternally a particle. It is never born, never dies and is self-occurring. No one creates it. Nobody can destroy it. It cannot even be broken. Even though an atom is extraordinarily small, it is still a mass that has shape, size and weight. Despite being in large numbers, the number of atoms is stable. The quality of each atom is stable. This theory will be characterized as Pluralistic Materialism. Each particle may vary in texture, mass, size, shape and weight.

2. Materialism that focuses on energyism: This branch contends that substance has not only mass but also human touch. It has energy. When it reacts with the human senses it will make human beings feel that there is mass. Energy makes things and events in the universe happen. This energy can be called by another name. This invisible energy is believed to be a struggle in nature and is expressed in the form of magnetic energy, electrical energy, waterfall energy, gravitational energy, plant energy, energy of human intuition and passion, et cetera. Human beings are struggling to overcome all the time. Each type of energy in nature is an energy of struggle or the desire to maintain existence (the will-to-live). Although energy is not visible, it is transmitted to humans, and it has sense, because it is the most intense energy and may help to solve problems through another form of energy.

Some energyism comments on the intention to have the power (the will-to-power). It can be noticed that a power expressed in nature is sometimes willing to risk its life to have a power over another unit. Especially among human beings, this is more clearly observed. People fight each other to maintain a leadership position, hegemony. This will make people try to develop themselves to have capability over others. It will create human beings who have capability over others, which is generally called the Superman of the future. Max Planck and some of current nuclear scientists say that we can separate atom into electric charge, which is energy. Therefore, all mass is composed of energy. This energy is not homogeneous, but it is a group of sub-particles of energy, where each particle cannot be further divided. It is called quantum. Quantum is the smallest unit of energy, which when combined in different manners can create things and events in the universe. Energy in the universe is so powerful that no one can determine its extent, but it should be noticed that it is not stable. Its quality is always changing.

2) ***Metaphysics, idealism branch***: The word 'idealism' in metaphysics and ethics is used with a different meaning. In ethics, an

idealist is a person who can see the highest goal of life and try to get to that goal. Such a person is called an idealist. In metaphysics, idealist refers to the one who studies what is truth, what is the basic condition of all things that correspond to each other or one another in human minds and emotions. This person is called an idealist.

Idealists consider the mind as the only highest truth. Substance is only a phenomenon of the mind: for example, the human body is a temporary phenomenon of the mind and a residency of mind. When the body is dissolved, the relative mind still exists. It perhaps returns to its original source. It is the absolute mind, which is the original of all things. Everything can be explained with the symptoms of appearance of the absolute mind. The mind is *dhamms,* that which has only a name but not a figure or shape. Only those who have wisdom will know the mind. Everything that we perceive through the senses exists because of the mind. Truth is mind and idea. Substances or things of which humans have sensory perception are real but they are real because of the mind. As it is known or recognized by mind, substance does not exist by itself but it exists because of the mind (to be is to be perceived). If anything is not realized, it will not say that it exists. It can be believed that God has created the concept in the mind of every human being.

Idealism is divided into three groups: ancient Greek idealism, experience idealism and modern German idealism. The details of some of these ideas will be discussed in this article.

Plato was influenced significantly by the philosophy of Parmenides. He developed the concepts of the 'world of ideas' or 'theory of form' from the 'teaching of being' by Parmenides. Plato believed that attitude of human nature consists of two elements: body and mind. The mind operates in three sectors. They are lust, hospitality and intelligence.

a. Lust sector: Lust means the need for physical pleasure, such as eating, living and sleeping. Those in whom this sector dominates over the other sectors are those become easily infatuated. By Plato's perception these people are no different from animals. They seek happiness by touching, like animals do, though the human version may be more complex or subtle than that of the animal.

b. Hospitality sector: refers to the feeling of the heart (that occurs without a physical cause) such as love, sacrifice, discipline and mercy when seeing others suffering. People in the hospitality sector are still with desire because it is their mundane needs of body which are possessed by the mind. These people are not worried about the material. They are probably willing to die rather than lose their honour. These people are higher than animal because animal does everything, regardless of anything.

c. Intellectual sector: Intelligence refers to reason. This mind sector acts with reason, which Plato considered is what differentiates humans from animals and all things in the world. Mind intelligence makes human beings want to know the truth. People who have a lust sector mind may do everything to seek knowledge. People with a hospitality sector mind may sacrifice pleasure in order to maintain dignity. However, people with an intelligence sector mind may sacrifice pleasure and honor for knowledge and truth.

These three sectors of the mind help us see a person more clearly—what he does, how he thinks, and why does and says what he does.

3) ***Metaphysics, Naturalism branch***: It is a philosophy that lies between materialism and idealism. Materialism believes that only matter or substance is true. Idealism believes that rather than substance, there is also a reality which has more truth than substance. That is the mind. However, naturalism functions to compromise materialist and idealist perceptions through its neutral view. Therefore, it agrees with some aspects of materialism and other aspects of idealism. Anyhow, the basic principle of the naturalist perspective is closer to materialism. Materialism is a perspective that believes there is no God. There is no rule above the natural and no two sections between God and earth. However, there are some materialism doctrines that are compatible with the teaching that God is considered an ideal one. This ideal may influence the natural human who desires goodness.

Ontology is a branch of metaphysics because it is a science of the ultimate truth. The problem of ontology problem is trying to answer what is the ultimate truth. Philosophers have used several different ways to answer that problem. These become the theory of ontology. There are three important theories: monism, dualism and pluralism.

Monism is a philosophical theory that is considers that the primary element is truth alone. If the mind is considered the only truth then it is called an ideal monism. If substance is considered as only truth then it is called a substance monism. If truth is considered neither mind nor substance, it then called neutral monism. There is only one truth: that is God. God is neither mental nor substance. Dualism considers that there are two primary elements: mind and substance. They are split into two groups—one, which considers that the mind has created substance and the second which states that mind and substances have come together from the beginning. Mind has controlled substance by knowing the rules of the substance. Pluralism proposes that truth has several units. These may be mind or substance, or both mind and substance. Pluralist philosophers believe that all kinds of things in this universe cannot be reduced to just one or two units. They should have at least a primary of three units or more because the universe is very complex. It is considered that the primary element of things is not just one or two, but four elements. There are earth, water, air and fire. Things can happen because of the combination of the four elements with different ratios. Many new things are thus created. All the things happen and then change because the ratio of the elements themselves has changed. The demolished state of things is caused by the disintegration of these primary elements. A primary characteristic of each element is always constant. There is no rebirth, no death. It is eternal (Pra Amornmuni Suwan Waratayee 1972).

Conclusion

People in this world have different beliefs which vary amongst local residents, cultures or the teachings of their religion that they respect in each country. Different thoughts, words and actions, especially about this world and the next, are then put forth. There are some people who do not believe that the next world is real. These beliefs affect the thoughts, words and actions of that person. These beliefs have been inherited for over thousands of year before Buddha was born. Even when he was born, these teachings of whether or not this world and next existed were being discussed. Buddha has enlightened and seen all things by their reality. He saw the circulation of birth and death of all living creatures. It made him know that the beliefs about this world and the next world not existing were wrong according to natural law. These wrong beliefs are called *Mitchatitti* (mistaken notion)

On the basis of Buddhist principles, when it comes to the world, *Ludjateeti Logo* (**world**) means anything that can be demolished is called the 'world'. This implies that the world itself will change and eventually disappear. However, if there are external factors to support it, the degradation of the world would be worse and the duration of the collapse and damage will be faster than if would happen naturally.

This world is a world of variation. There are individual differences in terms of the physical, social and economic, intelligence and habit. The sources of these differences are karma—what we have done in the past, whether good or evil. The result makes us born differently with the tendencies and habits of our previous lifetimes. The next world or *Porraloke* has two meanings: life after death and the place for life to stay after death. After death, the physical and mental condition of the creature that is born in a new place is that only the previous body has gone but the mind has not. As long as the mind still has desires, it must be reborn. It will have life in the new body. What will the newborn to be? What will the shape be like? It depends on their karma—what they used to do. Where the newborn finds itself, its new environment, is appropriate to its karma, great or bad, depending on its previous thoughts, words and deeds. It will be in the circle of birth and deaths until the passion is gone or it has reached nirvana. Then the true, happy, cool peace will occur.

Thanks to your dedication. Thanks to the organizers of the World Peace Congress 2010, all who seek peace, those who are not encroachments of body and mind onto mankind and other creatures, people who are all aware, whose body, speech and mind are all the while composed and all who come together in this project, both in this world and another world.

References

Dhammaleela. (2007). Monthly Year 7 Issue 81 August 2007 p. 38.

The Royal Institute Dictionary. (1999). Available at http://rirs3.royin.go.th/word19/word-19-a0.asp Accessed: July 2010.

Pimpun Tapsumatanon and Associate (mor por por.). *Philosophy of Education* EF703 (603). Bangkok: Ramkumhang University.

Pra Amornmunee Suwan Waratatayee. (1972). *Western Philisophy* Bangkok บรรณาคาร p. 316.

Dhammakaya Open University. (2008). *Introduction to Cosmology*. Available: http://main.dou.us/view_content.php?s_id=35 Accessed: July 2010.

Guaguin, P. (1897). *Where Do We Come From? What Are We? Where Are We Going?* Painting.

Harrison, E. (2000). *Cosmology: The Science of The Universe*, Cambridge University Press.

Pearl, J. (2009). *Causality*, Cambridge University Press, ISBN 0-521-77362-8.

Ryden, B. (2003). *Introduction to Cosmology*, Addison Wesley, 2003. ISBN 0-8053-8912-1.

Peace in Siam

Nuttarote Wangwinyoo

After the forceful evacuation of the Red demonstration from Rajaprosong Street in Bangkok in May 2010, and after the application of marshal law during the state of crisis, many Thai people paid closer attention to how such things could happen in the modern era of democracy. The crisis was significant enough that it threatened our sense of security, and the country felt unstable. Even though there were doubts about the authenticity of the Red grassroots socialists and their connection with the former Prime Minister, Mr Taksin Shinnawatra, the Thai Government's decision to implement a forceful evacuation was questioned by public opinion. The impact may have been the dissolution of one of our modern illusions: that one can independently live one's life without political interference.

While more public attention is paid to political debates between those who support the Red movement and those who oppose it—some of whom belong to the Yellow royalists, with anti-corruption aspirations—it seems difficult to discuss this split openly, either in public or in private households. There are many emotional attachments involved, which reflect the need to recognize underlying values and assumptions. In some Thai families, husband and wife decide not to talk about their opinion on politics, spending a lot of time trying to avoid mentioning anything that would stir up arguments.

After Thailand's crisis in May, plans developed for a peace convention to be held in Thailand, organized by a group called the World Peace Congress (WPC), founded and first convened in Salt Lake City in 2007. The WPC's leader, Rajani Kannepalli Kanth, is a visiting scholar of Harvard University who teaches in the fields of political economy and peace studies. The Congress was scheduled to convene from July 9 – 11, 2010 in Nakhonnayok Province, Thailand, and it was designed to embody, in concrete, grassroots projects, scattered worldwide, the Resolutions that had originally been proffered by the Congress in 2007. The objective was to set up an institutional basis for co-respective and cooperative peace between peoples, unmediated by state, government or politics (understood in their traditional sense). The final goal was—and is—'to achieve, as a binding precept, the Universal Renunciation of War as a means or end of social and political policy, now and forever.'

I was involved in recruiting Thai participants and panelists to attend and discuss various issues such as gender dynamics, military control, environmental concerns, indigenous peoples, racism and ethnic divisions, Eurocentricism and modernism, et cetera. Given the political climate, it came as a surprise to me that I found quite a number of people who showed genuine interest in attending the gathering, despite the cynicism and despair around the violence in Thailand. In my view, their willingness was proof that, in times of despair, people seek friends and dialogue in search of a way out.

By the time the event took place in July, there were about a hundred participants, ten of whom were people from India, China, Singapore, Nepal, and the US. In his keynote address to those assembled at the Congress, WPC Trustee, Kanth, called upon the group to 'review the nature of the challenge(s) before us' at a point which is 'one of the great crossroads of history, ' where we are seeing the 'systemic, spontaneous breakdown of the *ancien regime*.' After a beautiful opening ceremony and a special address delivered by Sulak Sivaraksa, Nobel Peace Prize nominee, the Congress proceeded with full engagement, while people gathered in various sessions to listen to panelists and share their opinions.

We enjoyed a lot of sharing and learning, and we especially benefitted from making new connections. Many were from the outlying communities of Thailand, such as the indigenous communities from Northern Thailand, and some were Thai Muslims from the deep south; some were from the central upper middle class peace-seeking network. Moreover, there were college students, professional artists and facilitators, professors and environmentalists, community workers and local forestry government officers. Such a diversity of social backgrounds helped enrich and intensify the expansion of people's worldviews. Each of us brought with ourselves our personal experiences and how we looked at the world. Because there was a healthy and friendly space for these worldviews to be shared, deep connections and understanding could develop, and we could hope to gain a better sense of one another's complex social living systems, and to see our own roles in the world more clearly.

Besides those general topics around which people met for discussion, the World Peace Congress suggested that we host a dialogue specifically to address the violence that had just broken out in Bangkok a few weeks before, in May 2010. At first, my reaction was to doubt whether there would be enough interest or enough courage to sit down and turn face-to-face, to engage the opposing sides in dialogue on such an issue. But we organized it anyway, and about twenty people showed up for the panel session. I was the host of the conversation, which was listed on the Congress agenda under the topic, 'Peace in Siam.' It took the whole afternoon of the first day to outline the conversation, which we opened with a simple question: *How can a Siam in Pieces be at Peace?* I suggested that everyone listen deeply to one another and share their concerns and feelings. There were some challenges during the dialogue when different opinions were expressed and confronted. But everyone tried to express themselves through their personal stories, to show how personal experience had shaped or correlated with their political views.

One person shared in the group that he was involved in hand bomb making during the Black-May uprising, since he was very angry that the military had used violence against his friends. His love for his friends got him involved in the retaliation process. The consequence was that he had to live with fear almost all the time. It took quite some time before he could understand his own pain and violence, and before he was genuinely able to forgive those who had inflicted pain. His account challenged many of us, as peace-loving people, to really face our own fear of violence and pain, and to acknowledge that avoiding our fears is, in fact, another way of rejecting our understanding of violence. We can create peace only by working through the pain, fear and violence within ourselves and in our society.

Another account was from a man whose friend was about to bomb commercial banks in Bangkok last May. He tried every way to persuade his friend to change his mind, but his efforts failed. The friend was too committed to his rage. So he could only suggest to his friend that he wear a mask to be safe from being identified.

Part of the discussion was how each of us dealt with the violence that broke out. It was a tough situation, and people engaged in different approaches, including demonstrating against the evacuation of the demonstrators, writing in public forums such as Facebook, and contributing to websites to gain public awareness on the issues, et cetera. In order to move forward and suggest new approaches, we came up with some conclusions, which appear in this volume as the resolutions proposed by our panel.

At the end of the Congress, I was happy to see that many people had arrived at a new place in their lives: refreshed, empowered, inspired and well connected. Our Congress might not have given us any certain solutions to Thailand's problems, but we gained trust and hope through a social conversation that can inspire crucial new possibilities for peace in Thailand and in the world at large. During the closing plenary, one low-ranked Thai forestry official expressed the culmination of our work, saying, 'I realize I cannot change the world, but I can change myself to be peaceful, because I know it's the only way the world can change.'

World Peace Congress 2010

Resolutions

Panel: Gender and Patriarchy

Presenters: *Seema Luitel, Anupma Sharma, Pongthorn Chanlearn*

The World Peace Congress believes in 'Building Peace from Below'. To that end, the Panel on Gender and Patriarchy proposes the following Resolutions:

- To facilitate formation of a Gender and Social Inclusion Network for advocacy and monitoring at county/regional/ international level, which is vital for policy influence and for the necessary advocacy on different issues, more importantly gender issues.
- To empower and involve parents/families of Lesbians, Gays, Bisexuals and Transgenders (LGBTs) to fight against stigmatization of and discrimination against LGBT persons.
- To sensitize parents and other stakeholders on gender and patriarchy as well as on LGBT through various communication channels (mass media, local/national TV channels, flyers, campaigns, radio, and street drama).
- To provide necessary advocacy on formulation of relevant policies and programmes for the participation of parents of LGBTs across the world.
- To establish that gender should not always be perceived as a women's issue, because the promotion of gender 'as a women's issue' might alienate men.
- To capture the information, experiences, progress, improvement as well as failures observed at the grassroots

level so as to have Micro-Macro level linkages for necessary policy influences and replicating promising practices.

Panel: Politics, Nation-States and Militarism

Presenters: *Padma Rao, Phongjarat Ruayram, Sirote Klampaiboon*

The military, army, politicians are none other than people from our own communities. The institutional face of politics and state and military must be replaced by the human face. Dr. Daisaku Ikeda, third founding president of Soka Gakkai International writes, "No matter how great the divide between our ideals and reality may be, there is no need to give up hope or accept this. Instead, the ordinary citizens of the world need to come together to create a new reality. The prohibitions on land mines and cluster weapons that have been realised in recent years are the fruit of such solidarity."

Our Resolutions:

1. Role of Military:

- Long Term
    - ❖ Abolish armies.
    - ❖ All foreign forces to withdraw immediately from sovereign soil.
    - ❖ Use military expenditure in other sectors.
- Short Term
    - ❖ Engage with army personnel at local, community level. Identify with army personnel at human level (e.g., He is Thai. He is someone's son, father and nephew).
    - ❖ Use dialogue to change perception.
    - ❖ Convert army tactics of turning community members against each other to tactics of trust, friendship, and inclusiveness.
    - ❖ Set up events where soldier is engaged as human without uniform i.e. joint student camps like Prem Tinnasulanon's 'Statesman' programs with Mahidol University.

2. Rights of Civilians

- Connect local Human Rights for civilians to International UN standards. Empower local communities with means of enforcing their rights and fighting against false charges imposed on them.
- Abuse of state power during emergencies must be monitored and controlled (i.e. watchdog organisations consisting of local community members, military personnel, young, old, outsiders, etc).

3. Speak Up Not Out:

- Encourage awareness in a multi-faceted way (all viewpoints) and discuss in every local forum (family, neighbourhood, community) under rules of respect for all views without censure.
- Individuals to use all forums of media and influence to exercise soft power of protest against force i.e. talk shows, peace yatras, etc.

4. Empower Humanitarian Assistance

- All neutral personnel in conflict areas i.e. Doctors, NGO personnel, etc. to be trained in dialogue skills, conflict area psychology and used for actively fostering cooperation between military and civilians instead of being instruments of the military.

5. Empower Individuals, Local Communities:

- Strengthen community unity.
- Use existing local institutions such as women's groups, schools, community and religious centres to build togetherness irrespective of diversity.

Panel: Religion, Morality, and Transcendent Ethics

Presenters: *Bhikkuni Dhammananda, Ritu Datta, Karen Ohnesorge*

During mindful consideration of the relevant WPC 2007 Resolutions in contemporary contexts, and in collaboration with WPC participants, the Panel on Religion, Morality, and Transcendent Ethics, propose the following action plans:

1. Advocacy for Peace through Individual and Community Spirituality

We propose that the 2010 WPC declare the pursuit of spiritual growth and inner peace to be an inalienable human right; that we declare the nurturance of peace, religion, morality, and transcendent ethics to be an inalienable right of families, tribes, networks, and communities; and that we collaborate as a Congress to provide global advocacy in these matters.

2. Venues for Awareness and Sensitivity to Build Religious Tolerance

We propose that the WPC design and implement widely-accessible spaces to sponsor ongoing exchange on religion, morality, and ethics to raise awareness and sensitivity; these exchanges could take the form of online testimonials to human goodness, oral history podcasts to document diverse faith walks through autobiography, printed materials distributed at very low cost, cultural programs, films and other media (art, songs, graphic novels, etc.) that can bridge language and literacy gaps, etc.

3. A Curriculum to Support Spiritual Growth and Religious Tolerance

We propose that the WPC establish a series of instructional workshops (sponsoring existing efforts and/or authoring new materials) all over the world, that promote inclusivity and respect; that focus on the transcendent elements of religions, beyond politics and faith differences; that evoke the mysteries of faith grounded in trust; that introduce daily practices such as prayer, meditation, communion, and worship; and that engage in a reciprocal process of design, so that content emerges from local, convivial networks. Children and young people, university students, health care and social service providers, spiritual teachers and novitiates, politicians, citizens, and others—all would serve as instructors, and all would constitute potential students. Examples might include: diploma courses or certifications in peace issues, educational materials in all media, shared participation in services and rituals across religions, games and activities related to issues such as love and compassion, instruction in daily spiritual practices for peace within, college conferences, and sessions at future WPCs that include children.

4. Personal Attention to the Work of Inner Peace

We propose that each one of us engage in the process of developing inner peace so that peace reverberates outward into society; thusly we give more power to the thought of peace, expanding peace consciousness.

Panel: Law, Human Welfare, Children and Other Species

Presenters: *G. Venkatesh Rao, Phra Thanomsing Sukosalo*

It is resolved that Law is an instrument of social change and human welfare, as it has brought about a great changes in the field of rights of Women, Children, Weaker sections, minorities, racial minorities, aged, unemployed, homeless, the physically challenged, for bringing reform in the areas of educational opportunities, health services, employment opportunities, dignified living and working conditions, Taxation, and retirement welfare etc. It is imperative for all states and Govts to constantly strive to enact and seriously implement legislation that will protect and promote the rights of these sections.

We propose that an annual audit be performed by review of relevant statistics, as to the progress of the implementation of these welfare legislations, by publishing the same and making them available to the people through, press, electronic media and internet web-sites.

Responsible Governments, all over the world have enacted and implemented social welfare legislation to protect the rights of these sections of the society, and to take care of their life and Liberty. If the governments fail to enact and implement such legislation immediately, it will only result in protests, social unrest, and sometimes even unnecessary/mindless violence and demonstrations.

It is further resolved, that the Thai Government has not done enough to enact and implement social welfare legislation for the protection of these above-mentioned sections of society in Thailand, who have no means of protecting themselves and/or earning a livelihood.

The following measures must be immediately undertaken:

1. Free and compulsory education to children below 15 years of age.
2. Creation of funds for juvenile detention centres.
3. Homes for homeless.
4. Adequate financial assistance to the unemployed.
5. Necessary welfare measures for the care and attention of the elderly and aged persons.
6. Welfare measures for the handicapped and physically challenged.
7. Implementation of learning projects for the youth and for their personal development.

Panel: Arts, Culture, Media and Communication

Presenters: *Sornchai Chatwiriyachai, Prasard Prathedrut*

World peace can be nurtured only by listening to each other and not by listening merely to our own voices. We only want 'evidence' namely 'words on paper'," but seriously, can we really count on those words? Words that speak about more words keep us from real understanding. The arts are beyond mere words and aesthetics is beyond logic or reasoning. Culture is a fertile ground where the seed of human compassion can grow and prosper. It is also a foundation in the collective soul of our ancestors. If we don't have our cultural roots, we become strangers of peace. Children learn how to love other fellow human beings through culture. Culture and art help cultivate inner peace. 'The heart that sings and dances can do no violence.'

- Children who want to learn about the arts and their local culture should be encouraged and supported.
- Governments and educational institutions should provide learners with open opportunities to learn what their hearts and minds demand. No student should be persuaded to give up arts or culture for whatever reasons conjured up by their governments or anyone.
- Policy makers should not allocate budgets and their resources based upon conventional economic indicators such as GDP, which prioritizes materialism and excessive consumerism. But instead they should consider and adopt GNH (Gross National Happiness) indicators as their policy rationale, with the realization that the arts and culture are the main contributors of happiness and civil welfare.
- Local community should be empowered to evaluate and determine the appropriate media content that will be publicly available in the community. The community should be able to reject any form of public media such as billboards, flyers, PR buses, local radio, cable TV and so which do not subscribe to the acceptable local values with ease if it wishes to do so.
- All forms of arts and culture that are not against local values should be encouraged universally. They should be treated with the same dignity anyone gives to their own culture. Past history should not be used as a reason to restrain or to banish other people's cultures.
- Indigenous cultures and ethnic ways of life should be cherished and preserved at all costs, for nations should regard these various cultures as the weavers of their own unique cultures and national identities.
- Dialogue and deep listening skills should be encouraged and embraced as the means to cultivate real human bonding. Authentic communications can happen when we are able to talk to each other and mutually uncover our own prejudices or mental models which restrain us from more deeply understanding ourselves as fellow human beings. Newly emerging methods of collaborative conversation such as

World Café, Open Space Technology or indigenous tribal talk circles should be explored and adopted as a means to hold conversations within the community. These collaborative conversations give people a chance to voice their thoughts and convey their feelings, their worries and their fears; but because talks of these kinds can be threatening for authorities, they are frequently sabotaged or discouraged. Governments and policy makers should commit to this mode of communication as an important stepping-stone for democracy and make sure no intervention occurs. Also they should provide necessary space and budgets to enable these kinds of conversations in all levels of society.

Panel: Modernism, Tradition and Eurocentrism

Presenters: *Tung-Yi Kho, Tian Song*

A. The Panelists and Participants in the Modernism, Tradition and Eurocentrism Panel, after careful deliberations, *recognize* that:

(i) Modernism and Eurocentrism, which consists of the belief in the universality and superiority of modern industrial civilization, contain de-culturing effects that undermine the autonomy/self-sufficiency of communities.

(ii) Modernism and Eurocentrism, by attempting to incorporate all societies throughout the globe into the modern industrial (capitalist) system, fosters an ethos of one against all in a war-generating competition for scarce resources.

(iii) Modernism and Eurocentrism furnishes us with a vision of a utopia with ever increasing levels of wealth and material and technological progress. This illusory vision leads us to pursue it at all costs.

(v) Modernism and its pursuit does not recognize the limits of the planet's resources. Furthermore, it is wrongly believed that 'Science' – modernism's most esteemed knowledge form – and high technology will provide the solutions to such a problem.

(vi) Scientific knowledge is regarded to be the superior and only universally legitimate knowledge system in the modern world. Its institution as the only legitimate form of knowledge leads inevitably to the marginalization and elimination of alternative, local knowledge and cultures.

B. We should let people know that:

(i) Industrial civilization is not the only way for societies, and it is not the right way; it is simply unsustainable.

(ii) The real problem is not how to 'develop', but how to halt such 'development'. If we cannot stop the process of industrial civilization, human civilization might not survive itself.

(iii) We need to revive a different type of civilization, an ecological civilization, in order to live harmoniously with others and with nature.

In order to overcome the pernicious de-culturing effects of Modernism and Eurocentrism, we *propose* through *education* to revive all forms of local/indigenous traditions and knowledge to inculcate in the young, an appreciation for the traditions of their ancestors. Examples: local song, dance, folktales, mythology, medicine and art etc. This can be done by creating opportunities to bring the young and elderly together to facilitate the inter-generational transfer and sharing of knowledge.

These can be pursued in less formal settings i.e. in the everydayness of ordinary living, as well as *institutionally*, i.e., through formal introduction into school syllabi, as well as the establishment of *alternative educational spaces* teaching place-based knowledge. Also, one could seek the production of *alternative media* emphasizing local knowledge and culture.

1. The fundamental way is education. We need to promote an education reformation, to make local knowledge a part of institutional educational systems, and to let local knowledge have as much legitimacy as that of modern knowledge.
2. Before we change the education system, we need to make use of all methods that may have an effect on the human mind, such as art, mass media.
3. We need to promote local government to establish local

schools, teaching local knowledge in the schools.

4. We need to produce TV programs about local knowledge, and air them in local public TV channels.
5. We need to establish a prize, grant, or foundation, to support artists who promote the idea of an ecological civilization.

Means: to establish grants or foundations to support these initiatives.

Panel: Science, Cosmology and Metaphysics

Presenters: *Kampanad Bhaktikul, Dr Art-Ong Jumsai Na Ayudhaya, Prasart Meetam*

The Science, Cosmology, and Metaphysics panelists, after careful deliberation, submit to the assembled Congress the following resolutions:

Recognizing that:

- The simple discourses given by most famous peacemakers do not seem to be practical enough in the present world.
- The current energy policies bring the world into wars of individual benefit, cause global warming, and expand inequality gaps and local conflicts.
- Different philosophical and religious concepts and beliefs bring about intrapersonal and interpersonal conflicts.
- Sciences usually focus on surroundings but not on the core of human beings.
- Truth cannot be exactly discovered in the universe because everything seems to be changing all the time.

In this impasse, we would like to adopt the following resolutions:

- That more effective methods be seriously implemented to build up individual's physical and mental happiness.
- That a new renewable energy policy completely without exploitation and environmental destruction be brought into effect. This will include new laws, political will, and involve social participation and social support.
- That the beliefs of the world's various philosophical and

religious traditions serve as the basis for moral teachings and guidance despite the differences between them.

- That considerations of the mind and soul be included in scientific studies as they are as significant as that of surrounding matters; after all, peace starts within us.
- That science education be developed also for human development, not only for feeding the industrial plant.
- That people take care and be mindful not to disturb the existence of other creatures.
- That we leverage world peace conference as an equal to the World Economic Forum, G7, etc. i.e. Peace be a goal as much sought after as economic growth etc.
- That religious leaders be allowed involvement as stakeholders in decision-making on matters that have global consequences (eg. United Nations Environment Program).

Panel: Kinship, Community and Convivial Relations

Presenters: *Pakorn Lersatienchai, Cynthia Maung, Lau Kin Chi*

Resolutions:

1. To collect, document and circulate understandings and interpretations of the current crisis in Thailand from the perspectives of various grassroots communities and different social sectors, especially those which are marginalized, so as to make their concerns and plights visible and communicated;
2. To seek support and solidarity for actions and inter-connections to aid victims of violence and conflicts, and heal divisions within communities and in society;
3. To address the structural, systemic and relational issues underlying outbursts of violence and conflict, and to end social inequalities, injustices and oppressions that are the conditions and contexts giving rise to outbursts of conflict;
4. To promote reduction of communities' dependence upon the state or the market, to strive for the spirit and practice of self-reliance, and to regenerate cultures of communities based on trust, care, tolerance and respect;

5. To facilitate connections and interactions among the many communities and networks with which members of the World Peace Congress are already involved;
6. To utilize low-cost, effective tools such as Facebook, websites or direct exchanges among communities to sustain long term interactions.

Panel: Race, Ethnicity and Indigenous Peoples: Burmese Migrant Workers in Thailand

Presenter: *Anchalee Ema Janchum*

Challenges

- Negative perceptions of Thai government officials and rural people towards Burmese migrant workers owing to the history of conflict between Thailand and Burma.
- Conflicts of different ethnic groups in Burma that continue into Thailand. Some people in Burma reject identifying as Burmese but instead identify as Karen, Kachin, or other ethnic groups in Burma.
- Migrant workers from Burma come under the responsibility of the Labour Department.
- The government officials use the term 'National Security' in order to control migrant workers.

Resolutions

- Reinforce good relations between Thailand and Burma, especially by using religion and culture, in which they share much in common.
- Reinforce the education of human rights, the respect of human dignity, and understand and recognize the diversity of ethnic groups in both private sector and government sector.
- Encourage local authorities to take responsibility for migrant workers in their areas, and to accept that migrant workers are part of the local populationin need of their attention.
- Push to change the term from 'National Security' to 'Local Governance'

- Encourage the migrant workers to participate in solving the problem at every level.

Panel on Peace in Siam

Presenter: *Nuttarote Wangwinyoo*

Destruction of Human Life Is Unacceptable.

Regardless of people's political views or their actions in following such views, all life should be protected, by any means, from being destroyed.

Responding to Violence with Inaction Could Be Interpreted as Accepting It.

This topic challenged the whole group to pay attention to how we felt about and responded to the situation. For some, doing something could also worsen the violence, and doing nothing but only observing can be helpful in toning down the violence, as well.

Structural Violence Needs to be Changed

Structural violence is both internal and external. Internal structural violence involves attitudes, values and worldviews in people's consciousness, such as 'hill-tribe people are valuable only because they provide cheap labor, and their culture can make no contribution to modern development.' Or, 'someone deserves punishment.' External structural violence is expressed in public policy and systems around which our society is organized and managed.

Structural Awareness and Conscious Living

It's equally important that we recognized our personal involvement with structural violence. Part of the reason it still exists, or even grows stronger, is that it relies on the complexity of a system in which people cannot perceive the reality of other parts of the system. This structural violence relies on the disconnection of the system's members. So we need to reconnect with life in all parts and at all levels so that the illusion that perpetuates the violence can be understood and eradicated.

Pain Healed, Violence Understood

In order to create a peaceful society, we need to stop running away from experiences of pain, fear and violence. This does not mean that we have to be mean and love violence, but that we need to pay attention, with our eyes open. We cannot judge those who are in pain and find no way to be healed. Pain unhealed or unrecognized is expressed in forms of violence.

Overcoming Differences

We need to study to understand the mechanisms that separate our society and find ways to reconnect the gap. Skills that deal with different views such as 'dialogue' needs to be practiced and served in needed situations, as a part of healing, expressing, and creating our society.

We Are the World in Change!

We recognize our roles and places in the social transformation process. No can stem this tide of change. Some may wish to reject it, but no one can escape from the reality.

Special UN Resolution

THE 'WORLD PEACE CONGRESS' – 2010, 9-11th July 2010, Nakhonnayok, Thailand, Resolves and Recommends to the 'UNITED NATIONS' to pass the following Declaration for all Member Nations of the UN to adopt the same by suitably amending their individual Constitutions or by enacting a special Law by their Legislatures for the said purpose of declaring War as Illegal and as a Crime against Humanity and Mankind.

'UNIVERSAL DECLARATION OF RENUNCIATION OF WAR AS AN INSTRUMENT OF STATE POLICY'

PREAMBLE

Whereas the respective Governments, through representatives assembled in the city of San Francisco, signed the UN Charter on the 26th June 1945

Whereas the UN Charter so signed had inter alia the following avowed objective for the creation of the United Nations Organization, which in its Preamble, stated that the people of the United Nations are determined:

- to save succeeding generations from the scourge of war, which twice in our lifetime has brought untold sorrow to mankind.......
- ....
- ....
- ....

Whereas in the Preamble to the UN Charter, it is also mentioned that the respective Governments, through representatives assembled in the city of San Francisco had resolved to combine their efforts to accomplish the above-said aims by ensuring the following ends being adopted and practiced by member states:

- to practice tolerance and live together in peace with one another as good neighbours, and
- to unite our strength to maintain international peace and security, and
- to ensure, by the acceptance of principles and the institution of methods, that armed force shall not be used, save in the common interest...
- ....

Whereas, even after 65 years of the UN Charter having been enacted and adopted by over 192 member states, the abovementioned avowed objectives of the UN have not been accomplished, and the scourge of war continues to plague the planet earth. And on the contrary War has further brought about untold misery to succeeding generations and has further created other problems like Global warming, disappearance of valuable non-renewable resources etc, which has brought Planet Earth to peril and its very existence is threatened.

Whereas the 'World Peace Congress' 2010, Nakhonnayok, Thailand has at its deliberations, resolved that in the abovementioned circumstances its most imperative for the United Nations to pass the declaration renouncing 'War as an instrument of State Policy' and to declare that the member states of the United Nations adopt and amend their Constitution and/or enact suitable legislation denouncing/ renouncing War.

Whereas the Member States of the United Nations are further expected to promote PEACE, by positive policies and practices in the form of educational aids to all children in schools and other media channels, and also by dismantling their Armies and Military establishments, destroying all stockpiles of Arms and withdrawal of troops in foreign territories. Further initiate talks of peace with warring neighbours or other countries where hostilities exist.

Now, Therefore THE UN GENERAL ASSEMBLY proclaims "THIS UNIVERSAL DECLARATION Of RENUNCIATION OF WAR AS AN INSTRUMENT OF STATE POLICY" as a common standard of achievement for all peoples and all nations, to the end that every individual and every organ of society, keeping this Declaration constantly in mind, shall strive by teaching and education to promote respect for this Declaration by progressive measures, national and international, to secure their universal and effective recognition and observance, both among the peoples of Member States themselves and among the peoples of territories under their jurisdiction.

****

Prof. Rajani Kannepalli Kanth
Trustee, WPC

Surasee Kosolnavin
President, WPC 2010

Venkatesh Rao,
Vice-President, WPC 2010

Tung-Yi Kho
Secretary General, WPC

Record of Final Session

Rehearsing Revolution: The Final WPC Session as Open Dialogue –An Edited Transcription

Karen Ohnesorge

On the Third and Final day of the Congress, all Panel Chairs came to the dais at the front of the Meeting Hall to welcome discussion of the Resolutions we had proposed. Where known, the names of Participants are indicated. Their words are recorded here in the hope of preserving and honoring a fair representation of the wide-ranging and improvisational Conversation.

Rajani Kannepalli Kánth: During this session we call for dialogue; this is a chance to discuss why we've been holding this Congress.

Participant: What is the importance of these Resolutions? What will the results be?

Rungnapa Surached: I came to the Congress seeking to become a giver, to find ways to give without destroying, to separate donation from development. I have taken on the local administrators' role, with the idea that we find great success without thinking but by doing.

Participant: I don't doubt your devotion—but how can we have a process toward resolutions, a way for everyone to express themselves, if there is no space for open talk about the resolutions? Light and Peace are big words; we just need the process or story. Do we need this resolution? Is the resolution the only way to peace? Some participants don't feel they have the space, because of the formality of the rooms—

Participant: We have to notice in our hearts, some word [that] we must observe—how we listen and respond to events around the world. It is normal for this moment of division to happen: the objective of the group isn't what we want as individuals. But we have come to learn something from the Congress, about what is happening in the world. If we hope to realize that we cannot deny we are, ourselves, among the elements of violence, we have to start from our heart. What we are doing here is to express our feelings; how we feel is important. Observe your mind to the core of your feeling. What has been growing in our hearts from the first day of this Congress? If we miss what is happening within ourselves, it is meaningless to think about world peace. We want to hear about the feelings we find inside our hearts, for the good of everyone.

Participant: We have questions, too. What can others get from this Congress?

Participant: Before I came to this Congress, I had been working on a local project. The Congress changes my perspective, and it will change how I do my project. I plan to go back to local traditions; even if we live within Western cultures, with simple changes, we can find peace. Today, I feel local communities have been asking for something, and this is the peace I've been experiencing.

Participant: I'm just a volunteer at this Congress, but I am feeling that I need to do something—maybe charity work to help others. After this Congress, what can we do together to bring peace to the world and to Thailand? Is there any process or plan through which we can help others?

Kanth: I would like Congresses like this to be held everywhere, many times a year. We're seeing the end of an ancient regime, which is under collapse. War does not serve ordinary people, but only those whose interests are served. We are now seeing the final demise of European domination; peace is one issue that unites the message.

Participant: Maybe the most important part of the Congress is just the chance to talk—we all get ideas by seeing how others work to promote peace— and we will spread the ideas.

Participant: For this Congress, I think many expected to participate in different ways. Some of us were seeking answers from this Congress, but what we got is different: We came to find an answer to the question, What is Peace? How can we achieve it? But instead we have learned and shared experiences together. What I like here is that we witness how the experience of peace is different for all people, and we can speak from the authority of our experiences. People tried to talk about their own problems, and when we find resolution for our own problem, we find our own peace. Some don't know the peace in people IS peace itself—peace as silence. Here, I feel Calm and Silence—I feel fulfilled. We can also help each other find peace by connecting with each other—talking about nuclear production, etc. But we have different ways to connect directly and indirectly, and All is interconnected. We should see the whole picture of everything—even though war is caused by our differences, we can feel change, because we are human and can feel compassion for others. This change is something that happens in our hearts. We don't know how to stop war from happening in our country, but we are here to find ways; we are here to share the same heart, the same feelings. I work to help others; it's not that I expect to change society, but we are small points who help create big change in society. One day we can make all people happy—I find my happiness when helping others. We have to work to best of our abilities. Everyone is interconnected, and we can create change from this kind of connection, and this connection will be strong one day. I am not influential, but I can help create change in this world.

Participant: I have felt at times that everyone hates me: I was the first in my tribe to graduate with a bachelor's degree. People have tried to tell me to be quiet, but I also feel we find our right to be free when we talk. Now I am the teacher of children. We say teachers must be good to children, and thus we earn the trust of communities. But we see mistrust now in the villages. For example, in my tribe we must sacrifice buffalo, but local administration doesn't like that, and teachers are caught in the middle. Thai people say—old people are set in their ways....

Participant: Maybe these differences are what create problems, but we cannot engage in the fantasy that we are all the same. And, in any case, fundamental samenesses are not sufficient to prevent conflict.

Participant: I wish to make a suggestion: I love the idea of this Congress. It should be held everywhere, but maybe not in the way we do now; do we need big air conditioned room and expensive resort? Will we understand conflicts in an expensive hotel?

Participant: We must keep in mind that we are bringing together people from different cultures—it is our wish to proclaim our solidarity with these resolutions, which are being written here in Thailand. Others have travelled to a place that may not have seemed safe due to current events. We have faith in our safety because of the work of local organizers, and we thank them for their generosity for arranging this space.

Kanth: These Resolutions will be put together as a formal document, in English and Thai, which we will give participants a week to review. Since they are summaries of discussions of different panels, we don't expect big disagreements. This spirit of coming together to look for hope and alliances should not be held hostage by political divides. We suggest that organizers continue to help with the process by posting photographs and other materials at the website, and by providing contact information so we can contact each other directly. The purpose today is to make full use of this facility and our opportunity—to feel enriched by our collective work.

Each in turn, the Panel Chairs presented the Programmatic Resolutions that had emerged during Breakout Sessions on Day One and that were refined during Plenary Sessions on Day Two. The Final Chair to present was Nutt Wangwinyoo, who Chaired the Panel on Peace in Siam.

Wangwinyoo: Violence is unacceptable; ignorance produced violence—We should set up a Peace Network by all means and methods, gather input, to change and work and share happiness. sorrow, and suffering. We should train one another in how to engage in dialog and accept who we all are; we should train one another in the skills needed to be force for peace within communities or families, basic skills in how to be caring, understand diversity, and bring the dream and hope of Peace to reality, even inside the bedroom. Peace is a skill that requires intention, assistance, and training. My personal feeling as a Thai who helped to organize this Congress is that I want to fulfill my needs to participate and interact, while I also respect work when it doesn't meet my needs. I believe the voices we hear today show us that we are learning. We have to meet and work against our feelings. Even if we don't fully understand, we can't give up. I am especially glad to see our youth below 35 years old; I appreciate their ideas, as well as the voices of elders. These Resolutions are only one way to summarize our response to World Violence. I support these Resolutions, and I hope to continue seeing an international presence here in future years; recent events could keep visitors away, and we need help with dialog no matter where we are.

One by one, the Panels' Proposals were affirmed by Acclamation by the Committee of the Whole. The Final Text of these Resolutions appears elsewhere in this Volume. Then the Assembly considered a Resolution to be addressed to the United Nations.

Kanth: Our next Resolution is the most important: it will propose to make War illegal via a United Nations Resolution. All People are created Equal; this legal idea eventually brought about Emancipation. For first time in human history, we will be proposing a Statutory Basis to say that anyone who makes war is making war against the World of Nations—the grounds for *Universal Opposition to War.* Such legal statements are an important way to take action for Peace.

G. Venkatesh Rao, *Congress Vice President, read the Resolution twice for Clarity. The Resolution to the UN, which also appears elsewhere in this Volume, was approved by Acclamation.*

Wangwinyoo: I want to voice a concern about the idea of disarmament, to ask how we might provide for the safety of the process, given the diplomatic complexities of destruction of stockpiles.

Kanth: Those procedural questions would ultimately be taken up by the United Nations in their adoption and support of the Resolution.

The Floor was then open for further discussion to take place.

Participant: We have heard that we are at end of old paradigm—what is the new paradigm? The Congress can also ask if we are conducting this work in ways borrowed from the old paradigm. What can we do to evolve into this New Paradigm? We have learned here the importance of cultivating peace within, very important issue. Perhaps the next Congress could provide tools and strategies to build peace from within.

Participant: I want to say thanks to the WPC. I would like to thank the audience that gathered to discuss many ideas—like Ven. Dhammananda's image of the three fingers and the one finger—which inspired me to learn what I learned here: to work in my local area with the thought that I will bring this Peace Congress to my area, to build peace locally. I have learned that any other knowledge and experience we share is a tool for spreading peace, for understanding oneself and others, which allows me to make changes.

Participant: I think this kind of platform is very, very good. It helps us know each other more deeply. We should make this happen more often. Society has many conflicts, and if we begin with ourselves and then form a community platform for spreading peace, then we can affect the whole world. Then good things will happen to our earth.

Surached: I helped to contribute the means to make this meeting possible, as did the owner of the Resort—everyone contributed pieces, and we put them all together. Each one is Precious. I came with the expectation of becoming a better woman: as a result of this work, I will be a better mom and wife for my family—

Participant: Representing my small community at this Congress, and joining scholars and knowledgeable people, along with our friends from home, has warmed my heart. Now we will go back to help our communities. Now that we have had a chance to talk with each other, we feel our thoughts are right; sometimes we couldn't find an answer to our conflicts, but in the meantime, we have had a chance to get outside our local communities, and we find things we can bring back—we make many friends, and we invite volunteers to our communities. Some had to leave the Congress today because of busy schedules—how can we extend this platform? Can we take these ideas and do more? We have felt that we were working at a very local level, but now the platform is at higher level. From the first day, during the panels, and at end of each day when we share and talk over our meals, to the last day when Dr. Art-Ong summarized our efforts with many ideas, we have felt that we have been on right track: we are not really different from in the world. To lead to peace, through love—within the self, then within the community—this is very good. For letting us find this answer, thank you for this opportunity, thank you to the Resort's owner, to the World Peace Congress. Now I know what World Peace is: Peace is Energy from the Inner Self, that we bring to Community. I can do good things for family and community, and this has been a time when we have kept peace in this Congress, in this temporary community. Now we can conduct a Peace Congress for the village where I am from. Before the 19th we will start looking for a way to set up this meeting locally. My speech is a little long because I didn't speak before—

Wangwinyoo: It touches my heart: the voice you express is from your heart, just as if you were speaking to us in your Karen language. You are not only Karen, you are a small girl with a big heart. All of us feel that the inner voice might not be heard. Peace cannot happen if we don't value each other, even shy voices; I feel that the end we need to reach has already come to our hearts, and the aim of making a documentary, and negotiating with a big organization, that is a separate story. But here we have already met our objective, crossing barriers of race and difference. This atmosphere has expanded my horizon to understand the complexities of society, to open my ideas and my heart. To the panels, you have really contributed. I express gratitude to those who have traveled from many lands. At the beginning, we didn't know who you were, but we believe in this mission and the values we express. I hope we can continue to learn from and support each other. We always could do things differently, and I appreciate you hearing both positive and negative comments. If more events follow this Congress, if I were to be involved, I would like to participate more in designing the program, provide more time to play, along with approaching serious issues. I want to know all of you more, your daughters, your sons—

Participant: Through happiness we make the world a better place; it is not only me who wants to change world, but other friends from other countries who have the same feelings as me—

Participant: I didn't intend to come, but through Tukta [Surached], I have been able to meet you. At home, one day it was my husband's suggestion to ask Tukta to come to supper. I knew she was working for the community, and I learned that Dr. Surasee would be coming. Here I feel I met good people. I said to Tukta that she has a big work load, but she contributes her time. I have learned a lot from her. I have learned many things here, and our conversation makes me think I can share things inside myself. I follow Mahatma Gandhi's speech—when I leave this room I must continue to practice.

Surached: I only did what I could to help. I am grateful to our host, the Resort that has taken good care of us; to the volunteer interpreters; to Surasee, who started the network to inform everyone of the Congress; and to everyone who is part of the Congress. I thank Rajani for providing this opportunity by choosing this country in which to hold the Congress.

Tian Song: For most Chinese, Thailand is strange place: we don't really know Thailand or what it's like. Most of my friends refused to attend this Congress—a professor wanted to come, and he applied, but his institution declined to support him. His own university discouraged him from attending because of security reasons. For most Chinese, who don't know Thailand, there are many barriers between us; but, as we were discussing in emails prior to the Congress, I believe it is very significant to hold this World Peace Congress in Thailand. At other conference I met a German professor who had married a Thai woman; he said Thailand is more civil than most parts of world. In Bangkok, the international airport is much the same as others around the world. This hotel, too, is just a part of the world. In a way, it seems very familiar, with the same smiles, but when you speak, I can't understand. I see monks and nuns here; in China, I have Buddhist friends with the same religion, but different dress. After three years time, I am glad to be able to visit Thailand again— this kingdom of smiles, of Buddhism. So this is right place to hold this World Peace Congress. I feel a little strange serving on a panel that challenges the ideologies of Eurocentrism and modernism. In China, when I state my ideas, people disagree with me—they say we have the right to development, and they think I want to stop progress. After such reactions, I feel surprised to find so much agreement here. This is a very good conference, and I think we should hold the World Peace Congress every year, so that this topic will continue. I appreciate this morning's keynote message, that if I want peace, I must get rid of *I* and *want*. And if people understand each other more, peace happens. I also want to thank all the volunteer interpreters.

Participant: I see us changing Thoughts into ACTION—this morning my friend said maybe we are all different, but in our heart we now all have some peace: This is good *heart* action.

Participant: I didn't know about world peace before, but Tukta [Rungnapa Surached] asked me to come. It is good to have this chance to know others. Basically I am good with action, not with talking. But I think I can change myself, and maybe this will cause the world to change—

Participant: I am glad that my colleagues and I could participate. On the border, we see so much suffering, people displaced from Burma by their military. To achieve peace and democracy, we have to struggle together. Through a Community of Peace, we can work together and go home to Burma. We are continuing to experience difficulty there.

Participant: I don't believe in absolute peace, but as long as we live there will be peace within us—so we can pass this thought to our children and friends.

Participant: Before I came here I was trying to find information about the Congress, but surprisingly I didn't find anything. The Congress should be on MTV, on Twitter.... It should be easy to find such a great conference that brings everyone together.

Participant: Facebook would be a good way for us to come together from around the world.

Karen Ohnesorge: We do have a Facebook page, designed to provide an open forum for discussion. We hope you'll join the Group.

Tung-yi Kho: I think—I feel more than I can express. This is third time I've been involved in a session of the World Peace Congress, and it is remarkable that over three days we see this kind of energy, the result of intense work, and spending nine hours a day in this room. It has been painful, but it got us to this point where we understand each other. I feel not only relief, but also joy. I hope we can take this energy and continue our involvement, because this really is a collective and continuous process. I had been about to take a break and throw in the towel.

Rao: After having said so much during the Congress, I feel a loss of words to express my feelings. Congratulations to Professor Rajani Kanth for conceiving of this; many have tried, but he has succeeded in focusing a range of people to give voices to world peace. Governments are very uptight, and people have pre-conceived notions; following their own policies, they are inflexible people. They may not have imaginative ideas, being so caught up in their own worlds. Here, we see the most fertile ideas—and we see thoughtful people expressing their ideas, and these ideas all have been translated into panel resolutions, which will make a difference because they will be communicated to people who matter. Dr Art-Ong's speech was magnificent, communicating how simply we can achieve peace. Here we are looking at simple, general, from-the-heart solutions. We see why peace is important, and we see how war will destroy humankind. Today, although we may be a small assembly, we have demonstrated extremely wonderful thinking. We will make a difference; it has started, and the excellent idea of submitting a United Nations Resolution is at the center. Some will look at this work immediately and want to see how they can achieve this. Sixty-five years have gone by since the United Nations established its aim to end war. Now, Common Citizens are placing pressure on governments, on states, who do less than they should for achieving peace. We are the people, and they are there for us, so we will make something happen. Tung-yi, you have brought a lot of spiritual force here—for the wellbeing of all. Thank you so much for this opportunity to express myself.

Kanth: Perhaps our greatest achievement here was our proposed United Nations Resolution. No, I'll correct that: What we've achieved is greater ... We are mammals, heat-seeking animals, and *sentiments* are of ultimate importance. I believe we will remember that our hearts and minds were joined here, and that warmongers will lose, because they have forgotten our humanity. We have all won here. I wish your nations all good things. We are adjourned until 2011, when we will meet again.